You will laugh. You will cry. And you will forever be touched by these heartwarming stories.
- Kathy Harris, author of "The Deadly Secrets Series."

With 42 years of classroom experience, it is obvious that Deb is passionate about teaching. Deb provides insight on ways to connect with kids that textbooks never teach. I highly recommend reading this book whether you are pursuing a career in education or personally know an individual with special needs.
- Marcie Komar (parent of one of Deb's former students)

Deb was one of my best hires at Claggett Middle School. It all came about when she called to enroll Lauren, and there just happened to be an opening in Deb's field. We told her to send us her resume. Long story short...Deb came in for an interview, and we were impressed by her professionalism and enthusiasm. Deb kept this going for all the years we worked together. The students she worked with were truly blessed. I am happy to call Deb my friend.
- Jo Mauer, Retired Principal of Claggett Middle School

Deb has always been a champion for her students. She builds long-lasting relationships with her students and their families. Deb's classroom over the years focused not only on quality instruction but also on teaching her students social skills and getting her students involved in community service projects.
- Jim Shields, Human Resources Director of Medina City Schools, Medina, OH

Deb Laneville writes about the Miracle League, a baseball league for individuals with physical and/or mental disabilities. I am impressed with the way she describes how the players in this league are different from players in other organizations. She describes how Miracle Leaguers know how to celebrate the moment, how to do a dance when the home plate is touched, or to celebrate exuberantly when a big hit occurs. They are not worried about the score or the ranking. They just did something great, and everything stops to celebrate it. I also enjoyed the way she talked about sportsmanship. Players, coaches, and fans all cheer for and support all the players. They realize this league is uniquely theirs, and everyone is an accepted part of it. Life Lessons make it clear that there is a lot to be learned from these Special Kids.

- Ken Richardson, President, Miracle League of Northeast Ohio

You Can't Make This Stuff Up – Life Lessons from Special Kids

Debbra Kay Laneville

You Can't Make This Stuff Up - Life Lessons from Special Kids

Published Independently by SPECIAL LESSONS LLC, Medina, OH 44256

This book is memoir-like, with recollections of experiences and events over many years. The names of teachers and students have been changed to protect privacy. The author has remained true to the stories and events that happened and what was said.

Library of Congress Control Number: 2023913988
First Edition,

ISBN 979-8-8523-2060-5 (Paperback)

Book cover floral artwork by Madeline Beck

Book cover designed by Wooden Shoe Graphics, Mt. Prospect, IL

DEDICATION

This book is dedicated to the many students I have taught. You all had a story to tell, and I am a better person because I was your teacher. To all my students' parents, thank you for allowing me the privilege of teaching your children. To all the future teachers, parents, and people I have not met, may this book serve as a guide along your path to inspire and give you hope. You, too, will realize that children with special needs are amazing and have many gifts to share.

CONTENTS

ACKNOWLEDGMENTS

Writing a book that is more a memoir of my life than any other form of writing is a surreal process. It covers my 42 years of teaching and has been years in the making. I'm forever indebted to my family, starting with my mom, who nurtured a love of books at a very early age, and my dad, who taught me to "hang in there tough" during my early teaching career. Also, thanks to my sisters, Barbara and Karen, who led by example as teachers and avid readers.

Thank you to my husband, Don, who has been my biggest cheerleader, editor, and sounding board. You read the early drafts and worked tirelessly to help me make this book better. To my grown children, thank you for all your support and encouragement; Lindsay for your editing/marketing assistance; Ryan for the encouragement, and Lauren for your occupational therapy work in my class and creation of Time to Dine with 109, which promoted life skills within my students.

Thank you to Kathy Harris, my friend, and author of "The Deadly Secrets Series," who always had helpful suggestions, positive words, and resources when needed. You lifted me up when I felt overwhelmed or discouraged. Your knowledge of the process of becoming a published author was invaluable.

David W. Taylor, Retired U.S. Army Colonel and author of "Our War: The History and Sacrifices of an Infantry Battalion in the Vietnam War 1968-1971". I can't thank you enough. From what started with a prayer, "Lord, please help me with this book," came my meeting with your wife and my friend, Sue Taylor, who said, "Dave can help you with this." Oh yes, he most certainly did and offered such great guidance and resources, taking the time to introduce me to key people involved in book publishing.

Betsy Guerrero, your imagination and creativity showed me how to make learning fun.

To Jo Maurer, the Principal at Claggett who hired me. Thank you for taking the chance on a newly relocated teacher. I called to find out about classes for my 8th-grade daughter and got a job at the school where I spent my last 20 years teaching.

Thank you to my paraprofessionals, some of whom helped me remember some of these important moments in my teaching career, and all who shared the journey: Ann D'Angelo, Barb Dash, Cres Elsener, Mary Jo Jensen, Kim Kinn, Ann Lakatos, Lori Leyden, Peg Mahoney, Beth Moloney, Jennifer Mosgrove, Nancy Myers, Michelle Nelson, Elaine Nerlich, Jill Paradise, Jess Rees and Diane Supan. You all became cherished friends. To other paraprofessionals that may have worked with me, I am deeply thankful for all your hard work and support.

Bill Roberts and Brandon Roberts, you were an inspiration for how to do the job with love and laughter. You came to my rescue when I needed your help and encouraged me on this journey. Thanks to the many other staff members of Claggett Middle School for your support. Whether it was participation in my monthly Time to Dine With 109, the annual Spring Fling Dessert Luncheon, welcoming my students in your classes, or just giving a friendly hello, I appreciate all of you. Thank you to God, who directed this teaching career and helped me write this book. All things are possible through Him, and I praise His name for helping me complete this lifetime goal.

INTRODUCTION

You can't make this stuff up! This is a statement that fellow special education teachers and I would say to each other if we had a story to tell. Sometimes we would pass each other in the halls, shaking our heads. We all knew the body language. Something crazy, funny, or heartwarming had just happened. We would then share a funny story or something clever that was said by one of the students. When you read these stories, know that every word is true. They are stories from my 42 years of teaching. There are so many lessons throughout the stories where I reflect back and realize many times the student was the teacher. Together, we learned a lot!

When I was studying to become a teacher, the textbooks did not cover real-life challenges and how to respond. Let these stories serve as a resource for others and a way to pay it forward to aspiring special education teachers. I often said, "It's not a job. It's an adventure." That became the theme of my teaching career. Come join me as I recount memories of my great adventures.

When I graduated from college with an elementary and special education degree, I knew I wanted to be a teacher who positively impacted her students' lives. I wanted my name to come to mind when they were asked who made a difference in their lives. This is probably the dream of every person going into the teaching profession, and I was out to change lives and influence young minds. I knew I loved the special needs population and couldn't wait to get started on what some might call a career. To me, it was my calling and what I was born to do.

During my 42 years of teaching, I taught preschool through high school, with the most experience working with middle school children with special needs. When I went to college, I thought middle school was the one level I would never teach. Still, I loved being a part of all the tumultuous years of trying to discover identity during students' "wonder years." In fact, I loved every age I taught and felt like they had their own special features.

I always felt that students with special needs had their own superpowers. Just meet any student with autism, and you will find that person is an expert in something.

Being a special education teacher was a big part of who I was and still am, and I felt like it was time to write this book now that I'm retired. These stories are about the students I taught. Most stories are humorous, heartwarming, or have lessons to learn. Some are gut-wrenching, and not every story has a happy ending. I hope you may find something relatable. It might be something to learn, be entertained, or find interesting. All the stories are true, but I changed the names for the privacy of my students.

CHAPTER 1

The Early Years 1970-1976

When I was in high school, I taught a summer camp program for adults with special needs. I loved working with them. Life seemed full of kindness and gratitude when I would give them a boat ride or show them a craft. The simple tasks became joy-filled accomplishments, and working at this camp gave me such deep satisfaction. The lessons needed to be broken down into small, simple steps. When I showed them how to create something like a tree made from a pinecone or an abstract work of art using a marble dipped in paint and rolled around on a piece of paper in a box, the crafts seemed manageable. Learning by doing is a good way to teach lessons to this population.

Another peek into the lives of people with disabilities was when I was a lifeguard as a teenager. I gave private swimming lessons to a girl with Down syndrome. She was a sweet and enthusiastic learner, and it was rewarding to see her accomplish the task of learning to swim. She was a good listener and trusted me to teach her how to swim. She went from being afraid of the water to learning to face-float and turning over to back-float. She learned some water safety skills as well. Her sense of pride in her new skills was a joy to behold. For me, the pleasure of teaching a student a new skill was something deeply satisfying. I had a boy in my group swimming lessons class who had a prosthetic leg, and when he would get ready to go in the water, he would take it off, jump in and swim away. I loved his positive attitude and felt like he was a brave boy. He was an inspiration to me. He just carried on like he was no different than anyone else. In his mind, he saw no limits. These experiences brought me profound gratitude. I then knew this was my calling in life, and I was meant to be a special education teacher.

I started at a community college in my hometown, and they had a program called "Human Services." I started taking classes in this area because they were interesting to me. To get this Associate of

Arts degree, there was an elective option to attend an experience-based program that involved a residential program for people with disabilities. It seemed like a great opportunity. This was like a student teaching experience, but I was only a sophomore in college. I felt lucky to have had this experience early in my college career. This exposure to real-life teaching let me know I was on the right path.

Every day I got to work with people of different abilities. I remember one boy who was non-verbal and had autism. When he took my hand and gazed into my eyes, I knew this was an area that I wanted to learn more about. I was sure he had something to say, and I wanted to learn how to communicate with him. I could feel the frustration in his gaze and knew I needed to learn more. People with autism fascinated me, people with cognitive disabilities challenged me, and people with Down syndrome delighted me.

One day I watched a man in this facility experience a grand mal seizure. He dropped to the floor, and I first thought I was witnessing his death. I was shocked and alarmed, not knowing what to do or how to help. The severity of this occurrence and how another teacher responded showed me how to deal with these events. I went from being terrified to feeling like I knew the necessary actions. Also, talking to those who worked there gave me a great perspective. One of the teachers there told me to trust my instincts; she thought I was doing what I was meant to do. Her positive words of support gave me confidence, and I felt empowered that teaching was my calling.

My university student teaching experience was terrific, and my teaching supervisor was a wise and gifted teacher. He had a great connection with his students, who responded well to his directions. My teaching supervisor taught me flexibility, to think outside the box, and to look at each student as a unique learner. Creative ways to reach students through music, movement, and helping others were ideas he used in his classroom. He knew when to use humor and when to be serious. He taught me to take time to learn from each student and discover what motivated them. These lessons became tools I would later use in my career.

Watching this teacher daily gave me essential insights to help students learn. He would look at the root cause of the learning or behavior difficulty we encountered and help each child meet his or her needs. He taught me to look at the whole child and ask myself if that child was getting his or her basic needs met (food, water, clothing, sleep, and shelter). If not, that could be part of the problem when behaviors arise. Helping kids get their basic needs met was an important early lesson that carried over my entire career. He taught me the value of using music to soothe, energize or connect with students. This all occurred in 1976 when Special Education was trying to define itself. On November 29, 1975, President Gerald Ford signed into law the Education for All Handicapped Children Act (Public Law 94-142) guaranteeing a free appropriate public education to each child with a disability. This was a hopeful time, and I was happy to be a pioneer in the movement to give all children a free and appropriate public education.

I graduated from college a semester early in 1977. I was offered a job at the university lab school as a long-term sub for a class of students with severe and profound disabilities. In this class, students did not speak, or if they did, only in utterances of wants and needs. I jumped at the chance and learned that progress could be broken down into tiny steps. Sometimes, even the simplest of tasks, like drinking liquids through a straw, were to be celebrated accomplishments.

It was funny that even at that level, students would try to manipulate the situation or do as little as possible when called on to perform a task. With lots of encouragement filled with accountability, I learned the dance of expecting a lot, praising accomplishments, but holding the students accountable for their actions. An example of this was a boy who was non-verbal. When he met me for the first time, he acted like he couldn't do anything. An aide had previously informed me that he could point to the correct answer when given pictures of the right answer, so I knew he was hiding his true abilities. He looked at me and smiled. I repeated my request to show me the opposite of cold, and he looked at me. I said, "I know you can do this, Nate, and we will listen to music after you show me." He suddenly complied. Music was a big motivation for him. This long-term sub job lasted for the rest of that semester. From early "con artists," I learned to raise the bar of high expectations using motivators to help inspire learning.

CHAPTER 2

First Full-Time Job Iowa 1977-1979

When I was interviewed for my first full-time teaching assignment, I was offered two positions. I chose the one that paid more. I was the first teacher in a new program for students who did not necessarily have learning disabilities but were then labeled emotional disabilities. The idea of being the first in a new position intrigued me. I felt confident that I had what it took to reach these students. Looking back at that first teaching assignment, I wonder who learned more, me or the 7th, 8th, and 9th-grade students.

Every student was given the category of "emotional disabilities." During the job interview, the middle school principal told me the hiring committee had been looking for two years to find the right person for the position and thought they needed a 300-pound, six-foot-five-inch man. Somehow, I convinced them I was the right person for the job, bolstering my self-confidence that I was "the chosen one."

I went to school to learn about handling all behavioral, educational, and emotional needs, and I was quite confident I knew what it took to reach these students. I had one semester of working with students at the lowest level. I thought I could handle the behavior of any student that came my way and get that person back on track. I was a lethal combination of naïve, stupid, and optimistic.

No one knew what type of student should be in this new class program, and the reason(s) for their assignment had fit someone's definition of "emotional disabilities." I was given eight students, six boys and two girls. My belief now is that these were the students no one knew quite how to handle. They were square pegs that would not fit in round holes, so they created a class, gave it a name, and hired me. It sounded like a good plan for a brand new first-year teacher full of hopes and dreams.

At first, it seemed like a dream come true; I was a new teacher, and this was a new program that I could create, call my own, and implement. I had theories, lesson plans, and ideas of how things would go in my classroom. No one gave me any real directions, so I attempted to create the perfect classroom. I had bulletin boards that had a reward system showcased, which was based on a money system. One bulletin board said, "Show Me the Money!" It had giant-sized replicas of One, Five, Ten, Twenty, and One Hundred Dollar bills. The posters on the walls were inspirational, the bulletin boards would have made Mrs. Avery, my Audio-Visual teacher, proud, and everything looked picture-perfect, straight out of the educational magazines. I thought I had the answer for everything. Boy, was I wrong! My plans didn't always go as I thought they would, but I have to say, at the end of the day, I always loved what I did and felt like I learned as much from my students as they did from me, probably more. These were my students, and I loved the challenge.

There were always situations that they never described in the college textbooks, let alone how to deal with them or that they could even occur. Every story is true and is, in some way, a story of success. Sometimes the success took a few years, and sometimes, success happened daily. The victories for my students reminded me of the fable of the tortoise and the hare. The tortoise won the race, and sometimes life in the slow lane is the best kind of life to live.

I learned from each of these students that no matter what a person's disability is, that person has many more abilities and gifts to share. Connections are more important than the content taught. Building a trusted relationship has to occur before learning can begin. These children are special in their own way. I feel blessed to have been their teacher. As I said previously, the children's names have been changed for privacy reasons, but the stories are true. I hope you find them informative and educational and that they open your eyes to the world of these wonderful children.

Matt

Matt was a tiny boy with anger management issues. The first time I saw this sweet little boy, I was sure that if I was patient and consistent with him, he would lose the poor attitude and comply with the work that I gave him to do. How could he possibly cause that much trouble? Here I was, a first-year teacher in a new program, starting at ground zero. The first thing he said to me was, "I got kicked out of my last school. I won't last very long here." "We will see about that. I am not planning on going anywhere, and neither are you," I replied. I had been expecting this tough little guy to have a hard shell, but I was sure I could bring out the best version of Matt. I figured I could outlast any difficult situation he might present and prove to him that I was in it for the long haul.

"We will see about that," he answered. He never seemed very happy about anything, but initially, there were no huge issues. I kept thinking about his opening remarks and knew I would have to prove to him that I was in this class and that nothing he could do would change that. I felt like it would just be a matter of time before I would convince him I cared.

For several weeks, we did not have any problems. I thought this was the end of the big showdown. I felt he would believe me if I just told him I wasn't going away. Did I mention I was young and naïve?

I was confident that he was making progress. Things were going quite well with this charming young man, and I could see he was just clearly misunderstood. That lasted about two weeks. Now I know there is a term for it: the honeymoon period. It was short-lived. Then one day, the dark cloud came over Matt's head, the winds started howling, and for no apparent reason, he decided he was not going to listen to anything I said. This did not bother me at all; I knew it was coming. It was the proverbial calm before the storm. I just figured something happened at home, and I would be the calm of his raging storm.

I had a specific behavior plan and knew that if I was consistent and fair, he would get back on track. He quickly went through the steps of my plan, and the veins in his neck bulged as his face got redder and redder. So much for that theory as the storms of frustration, need, and anger reached an epic peak. Suddenly, Hurricane Matt arrived. Books started flying through the air, and

17

his desk flew across the room, tossed as easily as if it were a pair of shoes. I knew he needed a cool-down area so I got him to my time-out room. This was a room that I felt quite good about because it had glass windows and doors. I could see the student while they were away from others, and they could cool down with the repositioning they needed to restore a calm demeanor. At that point, I realized sweet little Matt had somehow morphed into a 300-pound gorilla capable of slinging a large school metal trash can through the shatterproof time-out window glass. The whole class just stopped what they were doing and stared at the rubble in the room. I just stood there speechless. I knew I had to remain calm, but I felt my own heart racing in my body. Now what should I do?

The other students looked at me as I looked at Matt. The whole energy of the class was filled with electricity and dread as if the students feared a terrible storm. A shatterproof glass window had been broken to pieces. This was my first big test, and I instinctively knew the last thing I needed to do was yell, although I could feel my heart continue to race. I took a couple of deep breaths to calm down and asked a nearby teacher to come in the door to let the other students know another adult was there with them. I took another deep breath and went into the time-out room. It felt like I was going into the lion's den. I sat Matt down and put him in a bear hug until he calmed down. I quietly reassured him that I was not going away. He began sobbing. His whole being seemed to deflate as if it was a balloon that had been blown up too tightly. As I was sitting in back of him and gently crossed his arms and held them to his chest, I could feel the tension slowly leave his body. I was unsure if this was the right thing to do, but it seemed like he needed to be saved from himself. I had enough sense to have my self-preservation at hand, too, so I put him in a position where neither of us would get hurt. He did not fight me but seemed like a limp rag, with all his energy drained. We just sat there like that for a while.

"So, now are you going to send me away?" his quivering voice softly said. The pattern of his life had been rejection, and I understood that this was what he was expecting from me. "No, Matt," I simply stated. "You are staying in my room, and I told you I was not going away." That seemed to soothe him that day.

As the days went on, I realized there were signs that Hurricane Matt was on the horizon. I learned to watch closely and began to read these signs. Careful observation told me when the storm was brewing. I kept a notebook to look for patterns of behavior. His eyes would dart back and forth. He would start to rock. His hands would start to shake. The storm was brewing, and I knew I had to head off the massive force in his pint-sized body.

I tried to become more proactive and start my action plan the minute I saw the black storm cloud hovering above his head. This resulted in more good days than bad. On most bad days, we would have to ride out the storm, but I would always try intervention first.

I suggested counseling, and the psychiatrist he saw placed him on medication. The combination of counseling and medication, along with me looking for the signs of trouble, started to make an improvement in his behavior. For the most part, he came to trust me and knew that I wasn't going to go away. I think that was a new concept in his world, and there were days I felt he was testing me to see if I cared enough to do anything about it. We continued to have our ups and downs, but slowly, he began to trust me and knew I would always give him consequences. There were times he needed a break to regroup, and I acknowledged that with a suggestion saying, "Why don't you get a drink of water down the hall from the water fountain?" I combined these consequences with lots of praise. The need for a break and consequences with praise were very important to help him start on the road to success.

Matt wanted and needed parameters set for him and started to thrive under the day-to-day sameness of the classroom. Routine and structure were important to him. School became a safe haven with consistent expectations, and he slowly began to see that this was where he could succeed. There were days he wanted to be alone, and he would let me know. I respected that and told him I would give him space. Having a schedule and checking off the tasks that needed to be done gave him control over his day. Having a routine in a place that was safe and predictable seemed to calm him, and he became a very productive student. Sometimes knowing that someone will not go away from you when you make bad decisions is the first step to being ready to learn. Sometimes a person just needs to know that others care.

Kelly

Kelly was a girl in this class that seemed to have no friends. Her clothes were dirty, and her hygiene was deplorable. Other students in regular courses ridiculed her, and she was the target of much name-calling. She came from a large family living in a small apartment. There wasn't a washer or dryer at home, and she was often left to fend for herself. Once she began in my class, we worked on her grooming and hygiene. There was a washer and dryer in the school, and I taught her how to do her laundry to have clean clothes. We talked about how to make friends, what to say to friends, and how to keep friends. She flourished with attention and slowly started to make new friends. She also thrived on my attention and soon became a motivated worker in the class.

Everything seemed to be going quite well for her when tragedy struck. She was walking to the mall at night by the side of the road and was struck and killed by a car. When I learned of this terrible accident, it broke my heart because she had come so far and was so happy in life. What would I tell her classmates? How do you explain something so terrible to students whose lives are already so fragile? I attended her funeral, as did several of my students. It was such a tragic ending to such a hopeful story.

How do you explain that to a class of students who don't have very stable mental health? I found it hard to process myself and tried to be as open and honest as possible with the students. I tried to focus on remembering her smile, her laugh, and the hard work she would always do. It was hard to find the strength to deal with this horrific end to such a bright future, but I knew my students were looking to me for guidance. They saw me cry, and we grieved together. Other students started sharing their feelings of loss for family members and friends. The counselor was made available for students who wanted to talk. They put a beautiful picture of her in the back of the yearbook at the end of the year, with her happy, sunny smile. I told my students always to be kind to people because they never knew what life had in store. To this day, I think of her and remember the hopeful future snuffed out so suddenly.

Roberto

Roberto was the first student to show me that I learned only some of what I needed to know about teaching in textbooks. He raised his hand during one of my first lessons on the three branches of government. I was glad he was participating because he usually did not participate in class discussions, so I called on him. I was not prepared for his question, complete with a goofy grin on his face.

"Can I call you Sugar Lips?" he asked me. I didn't quite know how to respond. This was definitely not in any textbook I had read. Sugar Lips? Really? The class resounded with laughter, and I could tell he was waiting for an answer. Everyone looked at me with big smiles, then looked to see my response. Roberto wasn't trying to be a smart aleck; he just said whatever idea popped into his head. Roberto always said random things that had nothing to do with school. I somehow felt like this was a test of the newly minted teacher, seeing how to make her blush or see what kind of response she would give.

"No, Mrs. Laneville will be just fine," I responded. I tried not to look as flustered as I felt. I could feel my cheeks flush, but I acted like I wasn't fazed by it all. It was good that I had been in lots of plays and loved acting when I was in high school because I had to act the part of a teacher who was not bothered by that scene. Where was that lesson in my college classes? Nowhere was that scenario mentioned in any college text. That day I decided the ability to act was a prerequisite to teaching because no matter how you felt or what students threw at you, you had to act calm and carry on with the lesson. My training in high school theater would pay off in new and unexpected ways.

"Oh, ok then, Mrs. Laneville, it is," Roberto replied. Afterward, it made me laugh because I was taken so off guard by that question. He was a boy who walked to the beat of his own drummer. He seemed oblivious to the norms of society. When Roberto walked down the hall, he would stop in front of the girls' restroom and bend over to try to peer in. I would constantly remind him that it was socially unacceptable. At any given moment, you would find him picking his nose and trying to entertain any audience he could summon. Kids' snickers and sneers seemed to inspire him, and he had no idea how he stuck out, or maybe he did not care. It seemed he felt any attention was better than no attention.

Witnessing his blatant disregard for social protocols, it was clear that his first lesson had to be social skills. We brainstormed ideas of better ways to get attention and occupy his hands. For some of his behaviors, I just had to call him out and deliver consequences for when he was socially inappropriate. Sometimes I simply had to give him behavior rules because Roberto never considered his behavior as different or needing adjustment. We role-played many social situations, with me pointing out how his behavior made others uncomfortable. This was news to him as if Roberto had never considered that idea. He would walk down the hall, scratching his rear end or other body parts, and not think twice about it. Kids would look at this boy, snicker, and whisper. Obviously, these were behaviors we needed to address too.

Sometimes, I would look at Roberto and think, "Where do I begin?" It seemed like his laundry list of offensive social behaviors never ended. Addressing the inappropriate behaviors became more important than any academic lesson I could offer, so my mantra became, "Quit picking your nose, Roberto!" Slowly, he became aware of his indiscretions, and he stopped looking under the bathroom stall, scratching and picking. I made a list of particular behaviors that were inappropriate in public. Such things as "I will not pick my nose while walking down the hall. I will use a Kleenex to blow my nose." These were to become his first lessons in the rules of civility. I would write these little social hints on note cards and attach them to a ring he could keep at his desk. Having these things written down seemed like practical tools to help him learn what most people already knew at his age. We would role-play social situations as a class after I had worked individually with him, and we would role-play correct responses. We would read social story books as a whole class and practice ways to have socially appropriate conversations. I realized other kids had no clue how to behave in different situations. Everyone benefited from these lessons, and I would try to work in the language arts lessons of the day of reading and writing. Daily social skills lessons became the foundation of each day, essential lessons we had to deal with before any academic learning could begin. This was crucial learning for Roberto and had to be the foundation of all his studies.

These were not lessons I learned from any college class book but true-life lessons that were prerequisites for learning. Those might give Roberto more success in life than any math or social studies lesson I would give him. Slowly he began to use the lessons learned from our social skills role-playing and was able to initiate appropriate conversations. I made him a set of cards to remind him of what actions could be considered socially unacceptable. He kept this set of cards on his desk. He also had cards that described ways to deal with problems. Roberto could stop inappropriate behaviors independently or only require a silent signal from me about what we had discussed before during our training.

I held my breath as we returned to our history lesson when he raised his hand again.

"Mrs. Laneville?" he politely asked.

"Yes, Roberto, do you have a question?" I cautiously replied.

"Why do we have three branches of government? Why not just one?" he questioned.

Success, I thought to myself. That was an appropriate question, so I knew we were making progress. Progress had been plodding;

some days, it felt like he took one step forward and two steps back, but he was making progress. I was proud of his hard work and cooperation. Now we could get on with the academic part of our learning.

Zach

Zach was a quiet boy who lived with his dad. His mom left them when he was young, and Dad had to work long hours to provide for the two of them but always tried to help Zach when he could. Zach did a great job in my class and responded to the attention I gave him. One day Zach came to me and told me he needed to talk to me in private. As he told his story, my stomach cringed, and I felt ill. He had gone to the local pool hall by himself the night before, and an older man convinced him to go out in the alley, where he sexually assaulted Zach. I didn't know what to say, and my heart hurt for this sweet boy. How could something so awful happen to this fragile boy, and what could I do to help him?

I was the first person he told. I felt I was not equipped to handle this, but I knew we needed to take action immediately. I was the one that Zach trusted with news of this terrible transgression. I thanked him for telling me and told him we needed to file a police report immediately. I went with him that night after school. We met at the police station, and he told his story to the police. I had this terrible feeling that they didn't give much credence to it because he was a boy in a class called "Emotionally Disturbed." He was not very well-spoken, and the story was harrowing for him to tell. I tried to support Zach by telling him to say to the police exactly what happened. I felt anger but knew I had to remain calm and try to help him convey the details of this terrible wrongdoing. At that moment, I really just wanted to throw up. A horrible person hurt this boy unthinkably, and I wanted immediate action to remove him from the streets.

I asked Zach if I could talk to the policeman by myself, and he agreed, then sat outside in the waiting room. I explained to the police that this story had many details, that Zach had never lied to me before, and that they needed to investigate this occurrence. I could tell Zach was telling the truth, and it was up to us to get this person off the street. The police were polite, and we did all we could do for now.

I left feeling a little better about it; I was assured they would look into it and saw that notes were taken and promises made to investigate. I called Zach's dad and had Zach tell his dad what happened. The father was furious, not only with the situation but also with Zach, because he had been told never to go to the pool hall alone. Zach did not come to school for several days after that, and I worried about him. I got permission from his dad and arranged for Zach to meet with the counselor. My heart hurt for this child who had been so terribly violated.

Several years after this happened to Zach, the man was caught and convicted of assaulting several other boys. Zach continued to come to school and graduated from high school. I am happy he felt like I was the trusted adult but was frustrated that immediate action was not taken. It sickened me to think someone like that could be out on the streets, preying upon young boys. I worried about the long-term effect it would have on Zach. I hope today he is a thriving, happy adult.

Tom
Tom was a boy who came from an abusive home situation. His mother had also been badly abused and even hospitalized by abusive boyfriends. Tom would call them his dad, but then they would leave, and he would say his mom was better. There seemed to be a revolving door of men coming in and out of his life. He had little to say about some and much to say for others. His mother wanted the best for Tom, but she had countless relationships with men that were alcoholics, drug addicts, or very controlling. When Tom first arrived in my class, his mom did not have a boyfriend, and he was trying to make good choices.

I sometimes wondered what was going on in his head. One time I was talking about the division of power in the American Government, and he laughed at me. "Ms. Skinny Laneville," he whispered loud enough for all to hear. "I see pterodactyls that are going to eat your eyeballs! They will poke them out first!" Wow. This took me off guard, and I didn't know how to respond. He started laughing an eerily, strange laugh, like the evil villain who became possessed in a movie, the one that had just captured innocent people and delighted in torturing them. His eyes looked strangely unfocused, looking in different directions, and I told him I would talk to him later.

These strange outbursts would continue, and I figured out he was trying to see their effect on me. I tried to ignore these behaviors and reward him when he was on task and talking appropriately. This didn't seem to impact him, and I realized he had severe mental health issues. At times, his eyes would glaze over, and he would start laughing. When he was young, he had watched one of his mother's boyfriends try to set her on fire, so who knew what he was thinking? He seemed to detach himself from the here and now, and I knew his mind was elsewhere. He needed some dire help that I was not equipped to give him, but I always tried to treat him with kindness and respect. For the remaining two years I was there, he could function better. I would assure him that he was at school and he was safe. The glazed look and the weird laughter never did stop, but he did his work most days and felt safe. Hopefully, he felt cared for while he was at school.

Billy

Billy was the youngest of eight siblings. All his siblings had been stellar students, but then along came Billy. Teachers had warned me about him. People quickly told me he was nothing like his brothers and sisters. His reputation preceded him with stories of impulsive and erratic behavior. He was one of the first students placed in my class, and everyone told me how they were glad he was in my class and not their class. Before he was placed in my class, one of his famous episodes was when he almost blew up the science lab. He was legendary in the school for his act-first, think-later antics. Teachers would lament, wondering why he differed from his seven brothers and sisters. They all had been model, hardworking students. Billy had a quick smile and a curious mind. Being quite affable, he was the classic impulsive child who would do something, then think about it. He always wanted to see what happened when he... You can fill in the blank. There were many antics from this boy.

One day he decided to skip school. My classroom window was open, and I heard a voice yelling, "Laneville sucks!" I looked out the window and saw him grinning from ear to ear and waving to me from the passenger side of a passing car. The next day he got the consequence of in-school suspension for skipping school.

I said, "Billy, rule number one in the book of how to skip school - never yell and wave at your teacher while driving past her window. Rule number two - don't skip school." He laughed, but I knew he understood he had made a wrong choice that day by skipping school. He never skipped school again.

Another day he came to school smelling like smoke. I knew no one in his house smoked, and his mother would not allow him to smoke either. I tried the blunt approach, as I learned that was the best way to deal with his shenanigans. "Billy, why do you smell like smoke?" He looked at me momentarily, paused to consider the question, and said, "Do you want to see something cool?" He was a master of deflection, never answering my questions. Intrigued with where this was going, I responded, "Sure, show me." He showed me he had a pocket in his sock and could conceal a cigarette an older boy had given him to smoke right before he walked to school. Billy was always forthright with me, even telling me his bad choices. I just had to shake my head. A pocket in a sock? I didn't know such a thing existed.

This type of behavior was so commonplace with him. I knew that I needed to find a way to keep him busy and wanting to come to school. He loved to make things and see how things worked, so I asked the industrial arts, aka shop, teacher if Billy could come to his class which he agreed. So, during Billy's study hall, I took him to the shop class, where he began making a mousetrap car. I watched him closely, reassuring the shop teacher that having him in his class was a great idea. Billy was delighted when his car won the contest for the longest distance.

We planted some flowers at school and weeded around the front of the school as a class project, and guess whom I put in charge of supervising everyone? Billy was in charge, and he took his job seriously. If there was an errand of running something to the office, I would ask Billy. Of course, I would give him a time limit to prevent him from straying to other places in the building. Billy was a leader, and the students responded to him. I ensured he had plenty of hands-on classes and supervision when he went to high school. This was the winning combination for him. He was a hands-on learner, showing me that the path to success is not always in the books.

<u>Roy</u>

Roy was a boy who had great family support yet always seemed to make bad choices. The theme we worked on together was that actions have consequences. Working with him, I discovered he was impulsive and often acted before thinking. He failed to anticipate the consequences of his choices and actions so that the outcome could have been better.

Once, Roy was riding his bike close to my house, stopped, and wrote on my car with a magic marker. He drew a picture of a meme character and wrote, "Roy was here." Upon hearing something, I saw Roy pedaling down the street. Recognizing the new artwork on my car, I called his house and explained to his mother what had just happened. She was mortified, and together we decided he needed to pay some restitution, so she sent him back to my house with some cleaner. Fortunately, the markings came off. From that incident, I learned that sometimes requiring restitution is the best way to stop poor choices. At the very least, it gave Roy pause to think about how much trouble he had with his mom and how hard it was to scrub that marker off my car.

We spent much time looking at why he was making poor decisions, and his mom did a great job of adding her thoughts since it was also a problem at home. We figured out that he deliberately made poor choices when he felt pressured, stressed, or was seeking attention. He had two older brothers who were in sports and got all A's. Roy's poor behavior was his way of making his name known. I began to present different scenarios, and we acted out what actions should be taken. When given choices, he was instructed to stop and think. We used his poor decisions and turned them into learning opportunities of how it went wrong and what he could do to make better choices. Both his mom and I made sure we praised him when he made good choices, and slowly, he began to turn his behavior around.

In those two years, I learned a lot about students. Many kids in my first two years of teaching came from dysfunctional families. Kids no one seemed to care about, kids that had been forgotten or written off as not worth much. In those two years, I taught them to realize they had much self-worth and could be positive contributors in their lives. I hope the lessons I taught went beyond the tough middle school years. I tried to teach them life lessons to bolster them for the challenges of their lives. I wanted to teach them to be problem solvers so that they could become self-sufficient. I often wonder what became of all of them. I pray that I gave them the tools to prosper and face hardships.

When I resigned from my position at this school, an article in the paper said, "Debbra Laneville, emotionally disturbed teacher from Grant Junior High, has resigned." I laughed at that and joked that it would be an excellent article for my resume. It showed me how labels don't always get it right.

CHAPTER 3

Dream Job in Kansas 1979-1987

My husband's job transferred us to another city. I felt like these early years were excellent training grounds for my field. I interviewed and was hired in a school district known for the strength of its special education department. I was thrilled to teach middle school again, but this time I was teaching students with education difficulties, not students with emotional disabilities. I always get a kick out of, "What exactly do we name these categories?" The whole alphabet soup of special education labels was pretty meaningless, and I just wanted to know about each child. What are the child's strengths and weaknesses?

I would team teach with another special education teacher in this middle school position. She was a seasoned teacher and had a great handle on discipline. The students were now labeled EMR and LD, meaning educable mentally retarded and learning disabled, respectively. The kids were mainstreamed in many classes, and I taught them language arts and math. The other teacher and I were close to being polar opposites in personality. Yet, we maintained a good balance for the students. It was helpful to me to have another person in the position. By now, I was a mom of two children, a girl and a boy. I valued home and family and balanced my work life well. My emphasis at that time had been working with students with emotional difficulties; hers was with students with educational challenges. She was single, firstborn, and had grown up in a military family, moving around a lot. I was the third of three girls, born and raised in Iowa, and lived in the same house until I went to college. Sometimes we would team-teach lessons. Occasionally, we would teach our own.

Many of these students had excellent social skills, and their social lives were sometimes more important to them than anything I could teach them from a book. Part of my job was helping them find that balance. I became the cheerleader sponsor for the school, and they joined the pep club. We raised money for uniforms by having car washes, and they showed up on Saturdays to help. It was essential for them to be accepted by their peers. Two boys, in particular, were very socially aware and struggled to find the balance.

We shared a paraprofessional aide in our class, and I soon learned that Grace and I had many things in common. We both shared the values of family and religion in our lives and were on the same page in so many ways. Because I had lost my mother in my early 20s, I looked to this beautiful woman as a source of motherly inspiration. Grace became a valuable asset in our class and a role model for me in my own life. She was creative, hard-working, and deeply religious. She was a mother of four children, and I looked to her for parenting tips when our daughter was born. I deeply admired her sense of church and community involvement. The love of family and the support of each of her children was a lesson I would try to emulate with my family.

Certain people spread goodness, joy, and light wherever they go, and Grace was one of those people. She had been a kindergarten teacher before having her own children. Grace still had enthusiasm and creativity from those teaching days, so she added a balance to our class to help everyone (including me) grow and succeed. Grace was a calm presence in our classroom, had a great sense of humor, and was kind to everyone. The entire staff at our school just loved her.

Gary and Juan

Gary and Juan were both outstanding football players. They played for the school team and had many friends. When they were first assigned to our classroom, they were not happy. They both were such affable boys. Even when they would look straight at me and say they didn't do their homework, they would say it with smiles. I realized that football was their crucial motivator, so I became friends with the coach. I would have weekly chats with him about their cooperation in my class. They realized homework was a means to an end and started turning it in on time. I would go to their games and sit by the cheerleaders. I talked to their parents, and then we could talk about the game in my class. I praised them on specific plays they were part of making. They started seeing me as not just the "special education teacher" but the cheerleader sponsor and teacher who came to their games. Maybe being in my class wasn't so bad after all.

Hector

On January 28, 1986, a tragic event had a massive impact on my students in this school. The Space Shuttle Challenger broke apart 73 seconds into its flight, killing all seven crew members aboard, including a teacher, Christa McAuliffe. She was going to conduct experiments and teach two lessons. My class was very interested in the idea of a teacher in space. We listened in horror as the events played on the news, and the images left indelible marks on their lives; we had much to process. They were going to study Halley's Comet, and we had prepared by learning some information about comets in general. I was glad we were not watching the shuttle catastrophe live on TV. Still, the students heard about the horrific tragedy multiple times. One student named Hector asked me if he was going to die; if the explosion would affect us in Kansas. This was a student who had lost his mother to a car accident a few years earlier, so death and his own mortality were things he worried about quite a bit. When bad things happen in the world, kids take it very much to heart and wonder about its effect on their lives.

I talked to Hector and let him have time to talk about his mom. He started crying, and then I started crying. I had lost my mom quite young and shared my memories of her. I told him that remembering the good times with our loved ones can help, and memories can be treasures that we unpack from time to time when we feel sad.

I was in shock, but I knew I had a classroom of students looking to me for some understanding. "Well, this is a sorrowful day, but when anything sad happens, we always need to look for the helpers and remember all the good things that the people who are gone did in the world." I tried to explain the tragedy to my students while giving them hope, even though I tried to make sense of it. This was the second time in my career that I would have to grieve and mourn with my students, trying to explain things I did not fully understand myself. I learned it was necessary to let each student talk, either in the group or with me on a one-to-one basis, and slowly we began to heal. My job is to give them a sense of security in my classroom, knowing they are part of a caring community.

Marla and Jenny

Marla and Jenny were also my students, both beautiful girls. Even though they were both on an IEP (Individual Education Plan), and I was their language arts teacher, they had social graces and a high IQ in interpersonal and intrapersonal relationships. In this regard, they could blend in and add to any group of middle school students. The school nurse and I organized a health fair for the school and involved these girls in planning the event.

We called it, A Celebration of Self and Sanity and talked our principal into letting us have a whole afternoon and evening for the event. I wanted to create an event where typical students would inclusively work alongside my students to emphasize good health. This was inspired by a yearly event in the small Iowa town I grew up in, where every spring, we would have "The Dental Parade." It was a celebration that every child looked forward to for having good dental health. It was created by a school nurse decades before I became eligible. My vision was to have an event that covered health's mental and physical aspects. We had guest speakers, booths from various health organizations, freebies, and many interactive displays. Many of my students helped advertise this event by making posters. Marla and Jenny helped me plan a fashion show.

Along with some of my other students and the cheerleaders, they were models showing people the latest spring fashions from a popular store. It was a tremendous boost of self-esteem for these girls to be equal to the cheerleaders and the beginning of the acceptance they so richly deserved. The cheerleaders realized that these were just girls, like themselves, and not the special education students from Mrs. Laneville's room. This event served as the bridge to new friendships and acceptance. I realized it was important for the rest of the student body to understand that everyone is more alike than different. These activities greatly enhanced that understanding, and for the rest of my teaching career, I would try to create ways where my students felt included.

CHAPTER 4

Hello Michigan 1987-1989

When we moved again, it broke my heart. I would have stayed in the prior position my whole teaching career. By now, you are wondering why we moved again. We can blame or thank my husband for that one. He was climbing the corporate ladder, and I went wherever the "Company" told us to go. No, we were not in the witness protection program, although I would say to my friends jokingly that we were as an answer to why we messed up their address books once again. One friend told me I was now in pencil in her address book. Yes, there were more moves to come.

With this move, I was pregnant with our third child. With my first two children, I taught after maternity leave. After the birth of my third child, I stayed home for these two years and enjoyed being a full-time mom.

CHAPTER 5

On to Florida 1989-1994

Once again, my husband's job transfer resulted in another move. I grew restless and wanted to reenter the world of teaching. I taught both preschool and kindergarten. This was also when my two youngest kids were preschool ages, so sharing this experience with them was wonderful. I first taught three-year-old children at a church preschool. I had always taught in public schools, so being able to sing songs about God was delightful and a breath of fresh air. It was great fun to be in the land of pretend and adventure. I taught them many songs with actions, and I learned many songs from the music director to add to my repertoire. They learned a new letter each week, and I learned to create art projects with them that would reinforce the use of these letters. It was great fun; these preschool children were always filled with awe and wonder. Subsequently, I changed schools to be closer to my home, and this was also a church school that was forming. I became their first preschool teacher for 3-year-old children, then the first kindergarten teacher at the school.

One other teacher and I loved to take our students on imaginary field trips. The other teacher was incredibly creative and fun; I learned so much from her, and we became dear friends. In our classes, we would pretend we were going on an airplane invaded by purple people eaters. We learned to make volcanoes that would erupt in the sand and learned the value of free play. We had a pretend circus, using imaginary lions, elephants, and tigers. We had tightrope walkers and jugglers and learned valuable lessons about using our imaginations and creating something from minimal materials. The performances were given to the whole school in the sanctuary of the church, which I am sure delighted God. I carried these lessons with me for the rest of my teaching career.

Once again, I had an aide that would serve as a role model

for my life. Mary was an aide for my preschool class and my aide when I taught kindergarten. She was a deacon's wife and had served many roles in the church. Mary was both a mother and grandmother and had such a beautiful, calming presence. The kids would flock to her and give her their undivided attention when she read to them. It was a beautiful thing to behold. It was as if their favorite, sweet grandmother was there with them, always loving them. Also, Mary was an artist who painted extraordinary pictures.

When I became a kindergarten teacher, I had a vision for the classroom. I grew up in a family that went to church every Sunday. I attended Sunday school as well and knew the Bible stories by heart. I wanted something to greet these eager learners. In Matthew 19:14, Jesus said, "Let the little children come to me and do not hinder them, for the kingdom of heaven belongs to such as these." I loved the story, and Mary agreed to paint the scene of Jesus surrounded by children on a classroom wall. It turned out beautifully. I felt blessed that she captured the image I wanted in my classroom. "Let the children come to me," said Jesus, and Mary's painting portrayed that message of love. Mary later advised that she had never attempted such a colossal project, but my faith in her made her want to try.

On the playground, Mary and I had many deep conversations about faith, family, and our roles in the lives of these children. She was born in the same year as my mother, and it helped me to understand the world that my mom lived in when Mary would talk about the births of her own children. When she read to the children, she read in a soothing, melodic voice. Having her as my aide served once more as a role model for not only how to work with children but how to live my life. Her lessons of faith, creativity, patience, and love served as a path for my life and life's work.

One of my favorite projects was to grow butterflies and plant the correct plants for a beautiful butterfly garden on the church grounds. We learned the life cycle of the caterpillar transforming into a beautiful butterfly. When our butterflies were ready to be released, we could put them in the garden. The look of wonder on the faces of the children as the butterflies sat perched on my hand, slowly gathering the strength to fly away, was a beautiful sight to behold. We tied it into the hope of spring and the newness of life. To this day, I share this lesson with my grandchildren, watching the delight in their eyes as the caterpillars transform into beautiful butterflies to be released into the world.

These years taught me valuable lessons to carry forward when I would eventually return to teaching middle school special education. I learned to have projects that included art, music, and movement and find ways to connect with the beauty of nature. Children learn best by doing things and seeing the wonders of the world for themselves.

CHAPTER 6

Back to Michigan 1994-1997

Once again, we moved for my husband's job. I loved teaching kindergarten, and when there was an opening in a parochial school, I happily applied. The ability to combine so many senses intrigued me, and I wanted to continue on this path. Even though it was hard to leave the classroom I had created, I looked forward to new adventures.

One of my students in kindergarten had cerebral palsy and was legally blind, so I embraced having this little boy in my room. My principal was a nun, and seeing my resume with endorsements of regular education and special education, she later told me she felt I was sent from God. I felt blessed for this opportunity to teach in a kindergarten class of neurotypical children. Still, I also had a boy with special needs included in the class. I enjoyed teaching in an environment where we could openly talk about God's love and sing praises to his name. Also, having the opportunity to teach at this school was an exciting new adventure.

Charley

Charley was such a cheerful soul, walking fearlessly with his two braces and supports. He did not let the fact that he was legally blind slow him down, and he didn't miss a beat. Smiling as he made his way around the room, he brought joy to all of us, and the other children treated him as any other kindergarten student. At that age, there is acceptance of everyone and any disability they may have. I would read stories that included students that had various exceptionalities to them. Ours was an active, moving class, and I taught lessons through movement and song. Charley sang every note and tried every activity. When he would fall, I would help him up, and he would say, "Why thank you, Mrs. Laneville." Having him in my class was a gift; I was thankful to have that experience and be his teacher.

We would always have a music program and perform a show for the parents. At Christmas time, I wanted to do something extraordinary for the parents, so I dressed the kindergarten students as angels and drummer boys (I had inherited these beautiful costumes from my son's kindergarten teacher, who was my role model at this level. She had bravely taught us all that kindergarten children could learn complex songs while performing choreographed movements to the music). The children were all ready to go, and they all looked adorably angelic. When it was his turn, Charley went up to the microphone without a hitch and said his part enthusiastically. Seeing this and what it took to walk to the microphone with his stiff and awkward gait, everyone gave him a standing ovation. His smile was as wide as the ocean.

I was glad that I could be a special education teacher, teaching all the children in a regular education class. In those years teaching kindergarten, I learned the value of teaching with music and movement. Many times, we would learn facts through song. The movement activity served as an energy break and another way to connect learning.

For our spring show, we learned to sing the song "From a Distance" (1985) by Julie Gold and made famous by Bette Midler in 1990. The song's lyrics rang so true, and I choreographed hand gestures with the music so that when they performed the song for their parents, you could almost see the halos on those sweet children as they performed.

Creating these experiences gave these young learners a sense of accomplishment. I felt like God was with us, and I smiled at these beautiful children, given their performance with the innocence and beauty of their age. It warmed my heart and brought tears to the parent's eyes as they watched these kindergarteners perform. I would carry these ideas when I returned to teaching middle school.

CHAPTER 7

Move to Illinois 1997-2000

Sitting in the interview at the next middle school and being so nervous, I couldn't even think of the word "appointment" when I went to the secretary to tell her I was ready. I wanted this job but had not been back in middle school for several years and could feel sweat forming. I looked at her blankly and said, "I have a meeting with the principal at 10:00 am this morning." I was stammering. I really wanted the job, but I needed to calm down. I took a deep breath and entered the room with the interview committee.

The interview went very well. By now, I had some experience, and the principal told me I knew the answers before he even asked the questions. That made me laugh, and the interview felt relaxed, like visiting an old friend. I knew I could handle this job and loved the idea of teaching middle school students with disabilities again.

This area was predominantly Hispanic, and my students taught me Spanish swear words, so I could correct someone if they were calling someone a vulgar name. It was a class of mostly boys with a couple of girls, and two boys loved to goof around. They were not mean but would do anything not to have to do work.

Luis

Luis was a handsome boy that always had a girlfriend. He would focus more on being a Romeo than a worker in my class. When we started a mentor program in the school, I ensured the girl Luis liked was my mentee, so she would try to get him to do his work. This was a win-win because she wanted to help, and he listened to her. It worked for about a month until he broke up with her. I continued to help her find new ways to help others and not rely on a boy's whim for validation. I also tried new ways to motivate Luis and discovered that his dad was a great motivator and wanted Luis to do well in school. Sometimes, the simple question," Do I need to call your dad?" was all that was required. Dad was always available and knew how to reach his son, so Luis always came back ready to work after a talk with Dad.

Angelo

Angelo was best friends with Luis, and together they loved to tease other people. They loved to tease me. They were both very likable, although keeping them on task was always challenging. I found that if they had an audience to perform for, they lost their focus. I started having them come together and have my aide work with them to study for tests. Having them in small groups was also beneficial; finding students like Erica and Veronica to be in those groups was very helpful.

Erica was Angelo's younger sister, and she was unfazed by his antics. Erica's threat of telling their mom seemed to have power over Angelo. Veronica was the cousin of Luis, and the threat of her telling his dad seemed to keep him in line. These two girls became my allies in the struggle to motivate the two comedians.

Angelo loved to play basketball and told me he wanted to be on the high school basketball team. I loved hearing this because staying on the basketball team required good grades, and he knew I was the one to help him achieve those grades. Once he started playing basketball, he became a more focused student.

Salvador

Salvador was a boy with Down syndrome who was a serious, hard-working student. He was the youngest of five children. I knew all of his siblings were just as hard-working and supported Salvador. He was the one I could rely on to take a note to the office or run an errand. Sometimes Sal sat in on the test session with Angelo and Luis, and even though he could not handle the academic challenge of their work, he could sit beside them and complete his work, completely ignoring them.

I taught at this school for three years, and when I left, my aide and my students made a memory book for me. Each person had their photo on a page and wrote something to me. This is a treasure that I can look at and relive at that time. Luis said, "I know sometimes I act like a jerk and say stuff you don't like, and I just want to apologize. Thank you for helping me with everything, not just with work. I hope I get to see you again. Love, Luis". This touched my heart because it told me that underneath all the wasted time and silly antics, this guy knew right from wrong. He had so much potential; when he was indeed himself and not trying to perform for someone else, he was a great person.

Veronica thanked me for being so patient with her. She apologized for all the noises she would make when she was tired or not in the mood to do things. It didn't bother me, and I told her it was ok to express yourself in a way that was not rude or disrespectful. I worked hard with her to teach her to be a self-advocate, and these were her first steps. She told me to keep being the same with my new students.

Erica thanked me for all my help and said I was one of those people who isn't hard to fall in love with and that I had a big heart. I told the same to her and let her know how much she helped keep other kids focused and on task. She was the one with a big heart.

Angelo also said his thanks and hoped I would find students like them. He knew I always found them entertaining, even though they made me want to pull out my hair at times. I taught him for three years, and Angelo said I was the best teacher anyone could have. He also said I touched his heart in a special way. Wow. This was from the guy who rarely spoke his true feelings and was always quick to make a joke or act as a class clown. The picture he took was goofy to show that side of him. He said thank you for all the time you gave me and the funny moments like when my pants fell down. I had forgotten that little scene. He reminded me that he was attending his physical education class and had sweatpants over his gym shorts. It must have left an impression on him, and he thought it was funny. I was just glad he had gym shorts underneath.

I had a lot of fun with these students, and in the three years I had them, I learned that behaviors improved by limiting audiences to small groups. If there was another student that could motivate the students I work with, I asked if they would assist in teaching the student. We laughed a lot in my class, and I had patience with them though some days it did not feel like it at the time. Darwin D. Martin said, "A teacher's job is to take a bunch of live wires and see that they are well grounded." That certainly applied to this bunch. I really didn't know what impact I had on their lives in the three years I taught them, but it is true, as John C. Maxwell said, "Students don't care how much you know until they know how much you care." These little notes they wrote to me let me know that I had touched their lives, and I know they had touched mine as well.

CHAPTER 8

Short Stay in Indiana 2000-2001

As a result of my husband's job relocation, I applied for another job with students with emotional disabilities. I went to the job interview thinking there was no way I would take the job because teaching students with emotional disabilities was draining. I tended to take their problems home and think about them all the time. Yet, when I was in the interview, I really liked the principal, and this school had some precise ways to help the students, including a social worker on staff who helped meet their emotional needs. I didn't feel like I would be alone on an island trying to help kids this time. In fact, there was a whole team of support people. The students were on a highly systematic point system, with many positive and negative consequences. The existing practice that actions have consequences with a built-in, highly-structured system of rewards in place was very appealing. I would not have to reinvent the wheel. They focused on maximizing opportunities for success, so I took the job offer that day.

The students were from a tri-county area and had previously been in their home schools but could not be successful. I would teach high school this time, so we also had to worry about getting enough credits to graduate. It was paramount that I find ways to help them succeed and get that golden diploma. The program parameters were new for many of the students. We would start the day scanning backpacks for contraband or non-school materials. The kids had to enter the school through a metal detector, and the staff ate lunch with them, so we could ensure behaviors remained acceptable. They were on a points reward system and got to go on a weekly field trip if they met the established point thresholds. The students only knew us by our first names as a measure of safety for the teachers. I became "Deb" instead of Mrs. Laneville.

Each class in the high school was required to help at a local food bank once a week. We would all ride the bus together to the food bank, and students sat quietly on the bus until we arrived. The jobs they were given usually involved stocking the shelves. The task was simple, and the students enjoyed completing it. Some students had to look for expired cans and put them in the discard bin. No one was standing too close to another person, and there was enough staff to ensure students stayed focused and on task. This was a way of helping others and was one of the projects the staff social worker insisted everyone participate in weekly. All the students looked forward to the change of scenery. It was a great way to teach these students to be helpful to others and that giving back helps you feel better about yourself. This social worker was on to something, and I would use this knowledge later in my teaching career. Students thrive when helping other people.

Bradley

Bradley was a boy with autism who did not like to meet new people. I started the year off right and introduced myself to him before the school year started. Bradley said," I am not ready to meet you." I had been warned that I needed to take it slow with this young man. "Will you be ready to meet me next week?" I asked. He replied, "Maybe." But that day, he did not want to look at my face.

That is what I loved about teaching special education. The students have such innocence and speak the truth from their hearts. They don't always tell you what you want to hear but tell you what is real. They are totally unfiltered.

The following week, I didn't know what to expect from Bradley. I was warned that it might take some time for him to get used to me. The bell rang, and he walked down the hall with a big grin. I knew that was a good sign. He approached me and asked, "Do you want to smell my armpit?"

I laughed and knew this must be some sign of acceptance. I said, "No thank you; I really don't know you that well." From then on, Bradley was a delight. Somehow, I must have passed his acceptance test. Quite often, children with autism have some subject that they know so well that they can almost write a manual on the matter. He was quite the expert on a well-known brand of rubber-made products. He would walk down the hall, pointing out which garbage cans and other plastic containers were made by this manufacturer. He was very excited when he discovered the school had added another one of their products. For a reward, he would look on the manufacturer's website and bring in their catalog of products. He was clearly the expert on everything they made and would make a great spokesman for them someday.

Bradley loved to talk about "the pokey," as he would reference jail. When he was in time-out at home, his mom told him he was on house arrest. He thought that was "the pokey." He said to me that in actual jail, you were served bread with no butter. This fact seemed to stick with him because he would ask me if he would go to the pokey about three times a day. This became a game for us, and he loved to talk about "the pokey" and always wanted me to repeat the question, "What do you get at the pokey?" He loved to respond, saying, "Bread, no butter." When saying this, he had a huge grin on his face. The thought somehow soothed him, and I think he was glad he was not in the pokey.

Even though his opening line was a little unconventional, Bradley made an effort to introduce himself to me, and I discovered that laughter is a great tool that would serve me well on the job. It was fun to find something to laugh about with my students.

Samuel

Samuel was a quiet boy who lived with his dad. His traumatic brain injury as a young child left him with a damaged frontal lobe. Traumatic brain injuries can affect people differently, and damage to this area can disrupt essential processes. As a result, Samuel was often moody, with his moods changing from calm to stormy in an instant. He would get frustrated when he could not perform a task (usually a writing assignment), and he would quickly turn over his desk and throw his books on the floor. Samuel would start swearing and then immediately apologize. The first time this happened, it took me completely off guard, and I ensured no one was in the path of destruction. I gave him space and did not say anything. Watching his body tense, then relax, I could judge when he was soon back on track. He had very little impulse control, so if someone said something he took as a challenge to him, he would immediately shove them away. Yet, as aggressive and out of control as possible, he could be the most excellent helper in the class to students he deemed needing help. Also housed in this building was a program for students with severe and profound disabilities; many were non-verbal and in wheelchairs. When we had fire drills, Samuel was the person who automatically held the door open. He made sure all those in wheelchairs would be wheeled out safely. There was a girl in a wheelchair that Samuel would help at every opportunity. As a reward, I started letting him tutor this girl, having her point to the cards on her tray to use for communication. He would become this amazingly patient person with her. Even though I only taught Samuel for one year, I knew he could use empathy and compassion to help others.

Janice

Janice was a tough girl who acted like she didn't care about anything. She got into many fights and seemed to have anger management problems. The first time I met her, she said, "I don't like females, and I won't like you." I responded, "How about people? Do you like people in general?" She curtly replied, "Not too many."

This is what I mean about not pulling any punches regarding feelings. What you see is what you get, and I knew I would have to give Janice time. I started working with her, giving her plenty of space to adjust to a new female teacher. I noticed that in her free time, she loved to write poetry. One day, I asked her if I could read some of her poems, but she said she didn't share her thoughts. I then gave her personal time to write poetry after she finished her schoolwork. Days later, she stated, "I wrote this poem. Would you like to see it?" I knew this was a critical moment. "I would love to see it," I replied. I asked her to read it to me and discovered that her speaking voice was full of animation, something I had yet to see in class. Reading her poetry transformed her into a softer, kinder version of herself. I told her I liked her poem and that she was a good reader. I asked if she would like to do some reading for some younger kids, and surprisingly she agreed. I brought two second-grade students from a friend's class, and Janice read to them. Who is this new person? She was very kind to them, her voice full of animation and emotion, and she even smiled at them. This was a first; I had never seen a smile on her face. She started reading to these students weekly, and her whole demeanor improved. She became more outgoing and less argumentative. I encouraged her to start journaling her feelings and continue to write. Giving her lots of encouragement and support for her writing brought a slow and steady change in her. The fighting with other people stopped, and Janice became a great classroom helper in my class too. By sharing her reading, she became different and brought out a part of herself I was delighted to meet.

Roger

Roger was a boy who wanted to do the right thing but was impulsive with a quick temper. His dad was in prison, and his mom always seemed to be in survival mode as the only parent of six kids. So, I wasn't surprised when Roger ended up in the juvenile detention center for six weeks. I recognized that it was still my responsibility to educate him. It was hard enough to find work that interested him when I had him in my class, yet I needed to develop something for him in that environment. I knew he liked math and cars, so I started with many math problems involving cars. There weren't many in print, so I made them myself. I added story problems that had all the race car drivers he liked to talk about. The math work returned to me fully completed, so I based my language arts, science, social studies, and study skills assignments around cars. I decided the secret to his success was to teach to his interests, and then we learned to build on those successful moments.

I got some car magazines for him to read and made my own questions. I could make up math story problems, use magazines to inspire him to write or make up my reading comprehension questions from the articles. Doing this was a small price to pay on my part because he started doing his work. I always went to the public library and looked for anything car-related. Still, it did the trick, and he successfully completed his assignments. When he returned to my class, I was happy to continue finding car-related things and use car magazines as a learning tool. I learned that only some students want to do the usual activities, and sometimes you must think outside the box when teaching those hard-to-reach kids. It took lots of affirmation and telling him he was on the right track. He needed a tremendous amount of encouragement and support. Still, he became a happier, more productive student over the year. He worked on his temper and had better control of his impulses. These lessons helped him become more successful and make better choices.

Early on, I learned that you have to have a sense of humor in special education. This is something that has served me well throughout my teaching career. Some battles can be won with humor, and victories need to be celebrated with the child. You have to be able to laugh with the students and celebrate what's right with them. Everyone needs to feel wanted and valued. This was something that had been missing from the lives of my students, and with a lot of patience, encouragement, and just the simple phrases of, "I believe in you." and "I know it is hard, but you can do hard things." transformed these students.

Many of these students were so used to getting something wrong that they feared failure. It was essential to teach them that everyone sometimes fails, which is ok. That is how we learn. I tried to give them many examples of great people in history who had failed at first. I told them about the failures of Albert Einstein, Abraham Lincoln, and The Wright Brothers, among others. They were amazed to learn this. Later in my career, the concept of Growth Mindset was taught, where these concepts were part of a mindset making failure the way to keep moving forward. I took continuing education classes on this growth mindset idea later in my career. I was excited that I understood how important this was to my students early in my teaching days. At the time, I did not know it had a name, but I saw the need in these children who seemed so beaten down by life already in their young school careers. I wanted them to erase the fear of failure. I wanted them to see opportunities to improve no matter how many tries it took.

Janice became this happy, helpful girl. For the rest of that year, she worked with the younger students, reading and listening patiently to them as they read to her. This was the first time I discovered that most people like to help other people. I found that when I could put my students in a situation where they could help other kids, either younger than themselves or with fewer abilities, they became great teachers and happier people. Destructive behaviors seemed to melt away, and the promise of being able to help someone else complete a challenging task when they were done with their work was usually a great motivator.

Roger needed someone to believe in him and his good and find compelling things. I started to understand that sometimes, they are just misunderstood. Some kids march to the beat of a different drummer. Their brains are wired differently than ours. It doesn't make them wrong or right, but we must realize that not all brains are wired the same. When you enter their world and realize that their brains may be wired differently, you look for common ground and discover that you are more alike than different.

Even though we thought we would be in Indiana for a longer time, word came that we needed to move once again due to my husband's job. The next move was to Ohio.

CHAPTER 9

Longevity in Ohio 2001-2022

We moved to a wonderful town that reminded me of my hometown in Iowa, and I was delighted that I got a job teaching special education in the same middle school where my youngest daughter would be in eighth grade. Many people asked me how I could teach so many different levels, from kindergarten to high school. To me, it was easy. It was a love of children, and it didn't really matter the age. I learned some valuable ways to connect with students on a different level using movement and music. All levels provided amazing gifts to share and lessons to learn. This time I did not have a co-teacher but wonderful aides. I am happy to say that this was my assignment for the next twenty years. I retired from this school and loved all the staff and students there. The relationships I formed there continue through this day.

The Power of Classroom Pets

In this last school, I learned the value of having classroom pets. They provided so many benefits, encouraged nurturing, and helped build students' self-esteem. In many ways, the kids seemed to connect to animals better than to other people. Taking care of these pets gave students a sense of purpose and joy. Animals helped students increase sensitivity and awareness of the feelings and needs of both animals and other people.

Through the years in my classroom, I had bearded dragons, hermit crabs, frogs, guinea pigs, water turtles, and a baby snapping turtle. We learned that having two male bearded dragons in the same cage is never good. They will fight, and you will have to put up "the Great Wall of China," which I called the divider we had to place in the giant aquarium. It worked better having one bearded dragon, and many students loved to watch Blaze, later Otto, then later Spike, eat crickets, mealworms, and cut-up vegetables. They provided a great source of entertainment, responsibility, and pride as my students took turns feeding and taking care of these reptiles. They learned that all living things need more than food and water for survival.

We even made an activity of catching crickets as part of a math lesson emphasizing number sense, weight, and dexterity. It became a fun competition to see who could catch the most crickets. This was a great activity for my students who needed to be active and have something tangible to count. What better lesson than who can catch the most crickets, then counting them at the end!

When we had guinea pigs, they became close friends, and students could see how their actions affected the behavior of others. The guinea pigs did not like loud noises, so sometimes I got some students to use an inside voice simply by saying, "The guinea pigs don't like that much noise. They want it to be quiet."

The turtles provided a relaxing atmosphere, and I had several students who wanted to spend their free time just watching the turtles swim around. One student that had a hard time coming to school had better attendance once he got to be in charge of feeding the turtles. He was an animal lover, having turtles, lizards, and snakes at his house. Reptiles seem to be our connection and when our class inherited a baby snapping turtle, he was the one who took it home, promising me he would release it in the creek by his house. We inherited this snapping turtle when the principal asked me, "Would you like a snapping turtle in your class?" The obvious answer would have been, "Are you kidding me? Absolutely not!" However, this was a hatchling, and I figured we would be safe to keep it for a while. He explained how he found it in his swimming pool. We both deduced that a bird must have tried to carry it in its beak as prey and dropped it. Of course, I would take a rescue pet. Who wouldn't?

Class pets helped ease tension and provided new

connections to learning for my students. They gave comfort, provided a point of discussion with anyone coming into my class, and gave a sense of purpose to those who wanted to care for them. They added so much to the sense of well-being in my classroom.

Ongoing Learning and Assessment

I would have many different types of students in the early years of teaching in this school. I had students with chromosomal abnormalities, including XXX, trisomy 13, trisomy 18, and a student with Angelman syndrome. I had students with rare syndromes, and not much was known about them. I had to quickly learn everything about the challenges they might face for each new student I received. I would research each syndrome and feel better for the knowledge I gained, more capable of working with my students.

I even learned that there is another type of Down syndrome called mosaic Down syndrome. We had a boy in our school with mosaic Down syndrome, and while he was on an Individual Education Plan, or I.E.P., his academic path was primarily in the regular classroom. In the Down syndrome I learned about in college, I knew that a person had three copies of chromosome 21 instead of two, but in mosaic Down syndrome, not all of the cells in the body carry the extra chromosome.

At the beginning of the year, I would take a lot of time to find out what the parent's expectations were for their child. Filling out a survey with likes, dislikes, motivators, and whether the parents wanted a program for their child with a larger emphasis on life skills or academic skills was very helpful. Most of the time, I found that the parents wanted a combination of life skills and academic skills. I always worked hard to be very collaborative with my parents. It would never serve any useful purpose to be adversarial or to tell parents, "This is my classroom, so your child will do this...." I tried to help them understand that they were the experts for their children and that they were a great resource of knowledge. The development of the child's goals was ideally a group effort. This helped set the stage for a successful experience in my classroom. This was something I learned in my years of teaching, and it served everyone's best interests, especially the children I taught. Parents had great insights for their children; after all, they were the ones who lived with them on a daily basis. A collaborative effort was something I worked hard to achieve with all parents.

One way I could work on life skills with my students came to me the day an elementary teacher gave me a shopping cart. A local grocery store had given her two carts, and she gave me one. I asked her what she did with it, and she said she had kids deliver items to other teachers. I followed her lead and picked students who would benefit from these life skills tasks. One student would go with his aide to get the laundry from the cafeteria, put it in the shopping cart, and learn how to wash the towels. This shopping cart was used for many tasks, including in the regular classrooms, and I was happy to have a real-world tool to help my students.

Paraprofessional help

I started with three paraprofessional aides who would be with me for many years in this classroom. Each year I would try to pair off the woman with the student or students with which she would work best. Some aides preferred academic roles, and some preferred more caregiver roles. Starting the year off on a positive note, I would give each woman some sort of a survival basket before the first day of school. I would include things like hand sanitizer, lip balm, lotion, and chocolate. Some years I would write a clever little poem using candy-related words and attach the associated candy to encourage them. I would give them a binder of the pertinent information they would need about each child, making sure it was kept in strict confidence and on a need-to-know basis. I wrote out the classroom expectations and tried to start the year with the idea that knowledge is power.

We worked together as a team. This was a concept that I would reinforce throughout the year, having meetings to troubleshoot or give new information to them as they needed it. We always found something to laugh about, even in incredibly difficult times and situations that were both mentally and physically draining. We became good friends, as I always worked hard to make them feel like they were part of my team.

As the years went on, some of my aides retired, and some went on to do other things. I felt blessed to always have a team of hard-working ladies, and I tried to get them to understand that our job was to help students the best way we could. Through the years, I had many different personalities of people that worked in my room, and I always tried to take that important team approach. Some ladies had the strength of being detail-oriented; some were natural caregivers and did a great job caring for the daily needs of students. Some were very patient and some could work magic with humor. Some ladies were better in science, some in history, and some in math or language arts. As I worked with each woman, I tried to understand her strengths and support each person as she worked in my classroom. The team concept was one that I tried hard to implement, and I always tried to lead by example. If a child needed a diaper change, I would be part of the team that would help. As I got to know the strengths of each lady, I would try to pair her with a child or group of children that would benefit from those strengths. We would have team meetings at the beginning of the day to understand the needs of our students. I wrote a long and detailed list of expectations at the beginning of each year and updated it as needed. As the needs of students increased, so did the number of aides in my classroom.

I had six aides for the last 14 years of my career. When different ladies would say, "We make a great team!" I knew that I had accomplished my goal of building a sense of trust and teamwork. This sense of teamwork did not happen overnight but took lots of planning and many conversations. I am grateful to all these hard-working women who were my eyes and ears in other classrooms when sitting in another class with my students. We celebrated each child's success, pushing them when they needed to be pushed and comforting and empathizing with them when needed. Each woman had a love of the special education population and the goal of success for every child at heart. I would not have been as effective without them as a part of my special team. For that, I am deeply grateful.

Trent

I had a boy named Trent who was diagnosed with Fragile X syndrome and was always so sweet and caring to everyone. His home life was difficult, but that did not dampen his kind personality. He had some behavioral challenges that included being anxious or afraid in new situations, trouble making eye contact with other people, trouble paying attention, and trouble with hyperactivity. In his first year of middle school, he was wrongly placed in the class for those with emotional difficulties. We later realized that his educational difficulties precipitated his behavioral issues. When given the correct level of classwork, he became quite compliant and was much calmer.

Wyatt

Trent had a friend in the class named Wyatt, a sweet, hard-working boy with a lower cognitive ability. He was best at tasks involving physical labor, like moving boxes, sweeping the floor, and delivering packages to other classes. Academic tasks were difficult for Wyatt and easier for Trent. They formed a bond to help each other, Wyatt taking the more physical tasks and Trent helping him with the academic tasks. I would have Wyatt's two sisters over the course of the years, and happy to have such a hard-working family to help.

Tim (Meemie) and Dennis (Monty)

One of the first comical stories in this school I can recall involved "Meemie and Monty." It seemed like many of my students came in pairs. These were not their names but my nicknames for them for a period of time. They were buddies that had been in grade school together. They had developed a brotherly camaraderie and, like brothers, would not always get along. As sixth graders, they had a big transition before they were ready for middle school. They had been in school together for a long time and seemed to have a love-hate relationship. They each had their particular behaviors when they did not want to do something. Tim was a boy with autism and some cognitive delays. Tim had rigid ideas in his head of how the world should run. I think it included not having to do any academic work. His elementary teacher said she had a rough time with him initially, but by fifth grade, he was cooperative and did what she asked most times. This was not the case when he started sixth grade. I think it was like starting over, with me as a new person. He hoped maybe there would be new rules that included playing all the time. I had other ideas and was determined that I would help him learn and meet the goals of his individual education plan. We didn't even have a honeymoon period. When Tim was presented with classwork, he would scream at the top of his lungs and beat his head with his hands.

"I DONE, OK?" he would scream at me, then start trying to beat his head with his fist. I blocked that move to protect him. Self-injury was his go-to move when he reached the point of extreme frustration.

He would try to run out the door and down the hall. I remember thinking that it was a good thing I was not a first-year teacher because chasing after him did not give me the look of being in control. I called him a "Screaming Meemie" and told him sixth graders did not carry on like that. That seemed to fall on deaf ears.

I knew he liked playing with miniature dinosaurs in rice as

63

a sensory break, and we would use this as a reward. He liked miniature things like horses and other plastic toys I would find in the dollar bin of various stores. When he started losing control and hitting his head or trying to pound his fists against the wall or a locker, I would hold Tim in a safety hold. This was a training I had been taught that keeps both the child and the restrainer safe. While effective in preventing Tim from hurting himself, these controls were exhausting. The pattern of me asking him to do an academic task and him trying to hurt himself continued. I always made sure the academic task was appropriate for his level. I wanted him to know he could do work and didn't have to hurt himself to get out of the work or when he was frustrated. We discussed how it is ok to say, "I need a break." Tim lived with his grandmother, who was a powerful ally in my struggle to get him to cooperate. She would tell me we needed to make a believer out of him. I would keep this "believer" idea in mind at all times when I worked with Tim.

Grandmother fully supported my plan to help him succeed and said he was just testing me. Her favorite saying was that if you gave him an inch, he would take a mile. We devised a home-school report, and she diligently reinforced it at home. If there was a time when I needed her to give him a pep talk (aka tongue-lashing, as she would like to say), I could call her, and she would do so. In my book, she could be nominated for sainthood because she lived with this boy who could give everyone a run for their money, but she always had his best interest at heart. Together, we changed him from a "Screaming Meemie" to a cooperative boy who is now an adult. He did learn to accomplish academic tasks and became a very good worker. He remained focused and worked hard.

I always made sure Tim got his free time as a reward for hard work and let him pick out the activity he wanted to do. Now that he cooperated, he turned into a fun student. As he grew older, he became more willing to try new things. He started taking therapeutic horseback riding, and this helped strengthen many of his academic skills. It helped give him the patience to learn new things, and this transferred to the classroom. He is now an adult and lives in a group home, seeing grandma twice a week, once to go to church and once to eat at her house. He continues to be a horseback rider and has competed at the state level in different events.

The way Dennis chose to test me as a sixth grader was how he got the nickname "Monty." This is a name that refers to a movie where some men try to make money by taking off all their clothes. Oh yes, that happened, as he didn't have an ounce of modesty. Dennis was a boy with Down syndrome who had more tricks up his sleeve than any magician I ever saw. His elementary teacher warned me about his behavior, but I was absolutely not prepared for the stunt he pulled. He was the youngest of three brothers, and the family was very supportive of my efforts. As an example of his tricks, he was given a pretty high-tech communication device, and he hated it. Mysteriously, it came up missing. He claimed to have no idea where it went, and no one ever found it. When he didn't want to do something, Dennis just sat in the middle of the hallway, or the room, depending on where he was in the building. Trying to move him was like trying to move a mountain.

I felt that since I began my career with kids with pretty severe behaviors, I could handle anything that this cute boy with a mischievous grin could throw my way. I was a seasoned teacher by now, not a rookie, as my dad liked to say. Boy, was I wrong! Just when you think you have all the answers, a new problem comes up. Teaching special education has a way of keeping you humble.

One day during my lunch break, I was in my room working on the computer. Dennis had been at lunch, and the aide that was with him let him get a drink of water from the fountain. For some unknown reason, he proceeded to get his whole shirt wet. As he entered my room, I turned around and told him to change his shirt to a dry one (I always had a change of clothes for emergency purposes). Dennis had a big grin on his face, and I should have known something was up with him. I thought things were under control, and I resumed work on my computer. My back was turned, and I heard the aide shout, "Get your clothes on now!" Dennis had removed all his clothes and started dancing! I told the aide to shut the door so the other children coming back from lunch wouldn't see him perform. He laughed and refused to put his clothes on. I told him to put on his clothes; he continued dancing. I convinced him to go into the class restroom, and fortunately, no other students were in the room.

I called his mom because she was always able to redirect his behavior, and she got him to put his clothes on. His mom told me that he liked to test new teachers, and I had passed the test. I didn't make a big deal out of it and kept the other kids from seeing it and teasing him. After that, I always paid attention when he had that "I am going to test you" look on his face. This was another lesson that you won't find in any textbook or educational digest. Both Timmy and Dennis continued to test me during the first half of sixth grade. By the end of the year, the behaviors had pretty much disappeared, and by seventh grade, they were just Tim and Dennis. I was relieved that the Meemie and Monty show was over.

As seventh graders, they could be mainstreamed in science and social studies. An aide would always go with them, and we would focus on big ideas of the curriculum. The regular education students were ready to embrace these two students and loved to see how they would present their lessons. Tim and Dennis loved being in those classes, so I knew we had to make abstract concepts into concrete ones. The other students were always curious to see what type of project we would come up with for them to present to the rest of the class.

When they were studying Medieval knights and castles, the boys made an edible castle out of an inverted angel food cake and used green food coloring cool whip for the castle, with Hershey almond bars in it for the dirt and rocks. The land was molded out of brown sugar. They were able to tell the class about the different types of castles, and then everyone ate the cake at the end. It was a big hit, and I knew we had moved a million miles from the days of Meemie and Monty. These students were Tim and Dennis, and they were an integral part of the seventh-grade regular education classes in science and social studies.

Donte

Donte was a boy who, when you looked at his IEP, you wondered why he was in my classroom. According to the report, it said that his I.Q. was 35. I had never had a student score that low and wondered if the local school for the severe and profound, non-verbal students would be more appropriate. However, that was before I really got to know Donte and his mother.

Donte was a charming boy with a mom that had once been a teacher in a large metropolitan city. Severe Rheumatoid Arthritis had left her in a wheelchair, and she was quick to tell me there was a restraining order against Donte's father. She went on to tell me all the things Donte could do and that perhaps the scores did not reflect his capacity to learn. I understood that she wanted to give her son the very best education and her concern that putting him in a different school would greatly reduce his potential for success.

The first day he walked into my room, he walked in with such a swagger and infectious smile, as though he was campaigning for student council president. This guy walked down the hall like a VIP, expecting the paparazzi to be close behind. He would walk with a big grin on his face saying, "Hey, Hey Man! Hey!" and his good nature and winning smile became something that everyone looked forward to seeing.

Even though he did not say many words, he did manage to say swear words very clearly. One day he shocked us all by putting his hands in the air, as if he was a revival preacher in a tent preaching to his adoring followers, and shouted, "Praise the Lord, mother f___ers!" His Mother was quite religious, and

I am just not sure where he heard that, but he got the reaction he was looking for, as evidenced by the utter silence that blanketed the room. The shocked look on my face made him grin, followed by a mischievous laugh. His Mom later explained that, yes, he knew exactly what he was doing and saying.

Donte was constantly in motion, and hip-hop dance moves were his favorite kind of moves. You would think he was campaigning for President, shaking hands and giving the peace sign to everyone he met. You couldn't help but smile when he came down the hall. I began to realize he was quite capable of doing more than I expected and held him to a higher standard. I still see him in the community from time to time, always helping his mother with some tasks like getting groceries and carrying them for her. He smiles when he sees me and waves, saying, "Hey!" I smile and wave back. I learned that students were not always the sum of their reports.

Nita

Nita loved to mother everyone. She was a sweet girl, and she would get her work done early so she could tutor Greg. She was always my extra eyes and ears, telling me if someone was not doing what they were supposed to do. I told her she would make a great teacher. This girl only read at a first-grade level but had the empathy and compassion of an adult. She had a lot of common sense too, and she would always keep the boys in line, repeating things I had said before, like, "Dennis, you need to say excuse me." "Tim, you need to finish your work." She did this in a way that was kind, not bossy, and the boys sometimes listened to her better than they did me.

She was a new student from another state and had a difficult beginning to life, yet she remained a positive, motivated student. She was in my class for two years and then moved. I was happy that I had strengthened her reading and math skills and hoped that the next teacher to have this girl would realize what a gift she was to any classroom. I was happy to visit with her new teacher and find out that Nita found some more kids to mother and some more kids to tutor.

Greg

Greg was a boy that I anticipated would be pretty high maintenance. He was a boy with autism and was described as quite the handful in his early years of elementary school. I had met with his elementary teacher, and she said Greg was on a behavior program. His mother seemed like a warm and caring person, and you could tell she wanted only the best for her child. She was nervous about Greg coming to middle school.

She wanted to make sure that the teachers at the middle school would be as caring and dedicated as they were in the elementary school. She had three other younger children; two boys and a baby girl. Greg was her firstborn, and she wanted to make sure there would be a smooth transition. Later, she told me she feared that he would go back to the days of time-outs, running, and hitting. It was written in his I.E.P. to continue a system of rewarding him with twenty pennies each day, allocating a few for each task. This system was very important to his mom, and I was determined to make sure I would do it every day. If he would get twenty pennies, then he would pick out a miniature race car that was provided by his mom. He would take one race car home each day, and when he was out of them at school, Mom would send the same ones in again. This system had been successful in elementary school, and I wanted to continue the success in middle school. The members of the elementary staff explained how far Greg had come. They didn't want any regression in the new school. It sounded like a lot of work to me, but I was certainly willing to help him in any way I could.

In the first week of school, I noticed he was keenly aware of the sounds of things. Greg loved the sound of the custodian's floor-cleaning machine, which he ran at the end of the day. He could hear the saws in the modular tech room when I heard nothing. He would just tune into these sounds and stop and listen. Greg liked the hum of the fan, the ringing of the bell between classes, and the singing of the choir across the hall from my room. These sounds seemed to make him very happy. I gave Greg a water bottle filled with glitter and water, and he used it as a sensory tool. I found a squishy ball that made a rattling noise when this amazing boy with finely tuned hearing shook it.

The penny system was an excellent plan for him, and it wasn't at all hard to assign numbers to tasks and have him count the pennies at the end of the day. Greg loved the ritual of counting, flipping each penny on the head's side as he counted. He was a child that always was in a good mood. I never saw him sad or crabby. Greg was the sunshine in our room, even on a cloudy day. There would always be a smile on his face, and he would always be delighted or thrilled about something.

Often it was a little thing that I would take for granted until Greg would point out what a cool noise it made. It could be the rain hitting the window panes or the bell between classes. In my class, I had one full-time aide and three other ladies who followed other students to mainstream classes. Greg charmed us all by his sensitivity to various sounds. One thing Greg liked was the lanyard that each of the staff members wore, and because we all had keys with our lanyards, he said they made cool noises. He loved it so much that we decided to get him his own lanyard. Greg would shake the keys and say, "I love that noise." He would come up to the adults and say, "Listen to this. I love that sound." In some classes, he would bring a squeeze ball and listen to the sound it made. He was told he had to take his "quiet ball" instead of his lanyard with keys if that bothered the teacher in that class.

At the end of his sixth-grade year, Greg got to go on a field trip to the indoor swimming pool at the high school. He once had a bad experience in the water, and he was very hesitant about it. His mom was unsure about sending him, but I assured her I would be his personal lifeguard and stay by his side the whole time. In high school, I had been a lifeguard, so I was confident in my abilities to keep him safe.

I showed him how to swish the water and make it sound like a washing machine. He loved the sound of the washing machine at home, according to his mom, so I wanted to show him how being in the water could be fun. For the rest of the time, he was content to make the washing machine sound and had a lot of fun in the water.

As a seventh grader, we decided to put him in the choir. He loved the sounds of things so much and really seemed to tune into the music. For the first performance, I talked to the choir teacher, and she and I both didn't know how Greg would handle a performance at night for the parents, but we both agreed to let him try. A very nice boy, who later would become a choir teacher himself, took Greg under his wing and showed him where to stand and what actions to do. I was in the audience close by, waiting to see if I needed to help. Greg sang, did all the hand motions, and followed the lead of this boy. After that, we all knew Greg could handle any choir concert at any time. His parents, grandma, aunt, brothers, and sister came to watch him. This was the first time he had ever been involved in anything like this concert and pride filled their eyes as they clapped for him. In eighth grade, he continued to be in the choir, and the director was delighted to have him participate. Greg's unbridled enthusiasm was contagious, and he would jump up and down when he saw the choir director in the hall, shouting, "Hi, Mrs. Carrington!"

She would jump up and down and say, "Hi, Greg!" It would be a daily routine that they both looked forward to each day. She realized what a joy this boy was to have in class. His zest for music was contagious, and students seemed to reach a new level of passion when he was with the group.

Greg taught me the gift of listening to the quiet and hearing beautiful sounds. He heard things that I didn't even notice until he pointed out the "cool noises." Now, in the summer, I can sit on my back deck and listen to all the beautiful cool noises made by the frogs, the birds, the hummingbirds, and even the leaves rustling in the breeze. I am more aware of each and every sound and enjoy the cool noises, too, thanks to an awareness-heightened ray of sunshine named Greg.

Annette

Annette was a beautiful girl that had a pitch-perfect singing voice. She would sing all the time, but because she only wanted to sing what she wanted to sing, she was not successful in the choir. She was a girl with autism who had a lot of sensory needs. Annette did not like it when other people sang or even talked, so she wore headphones all the time. I knew she was very smart but somewhat devious. She would observe other people and would know how to push their buttons to create chaos. An example was when she tried to grab food off the table when we were making brownies as a class, which upset one of my other students. She laughed, and I had to try to figure out how to get her to make good choices. It required a one-on-one aide who would need to safeguard her from actions that could be harmful to herself and others. An example is that we were told to keep scissors away from her as she would cut other people's hair, according to her elementary teacher. We always had her sit at a table by herself when she used scissors with her aide sitting next to her to ensure she did not cut herself.

I created a very structured system for her that included attending some regular education classes. She was very successful in them, and when I would give her a quiz on what she had learned, she always scored high marks. She would get breaks after short work periods to play games on pbskids.org because that was the site her mother allowed her to access. It was always a balance of working hard, then taking a break, but I felt like she made great gains in the year she was in my class.

Chase

Chase was a boy in my class that I first met as a fifth grader. I would have him in my class the next year, and his mom was nervous about what the transition would look like for him when he went to middle school. I appreciated her partnership right away as I attended his annual review, helping to write the goals that would carry over to middle school. She was very articulate and explained his early history to me. She said that when he was eight months old, a blood clot went to his brain, and he then had a stroke. This damaged the left side of his body. He was on feeding machines for the first few years of his life. The stroke left the right side of his body damaged, so he could not use his right arm, right leg, or the right sides of each eye. He then became epileptic and would have horrible seizures. As his mom was telling this story, I marveled at her strength and resilience. As a mother of three healthy children, I could not begin to imagine all the challenges she faced. She rattled off all the medicines they used, and I marveled at how she remembered all of this.

A decision was made to remove the dead part of his brain that was causing all the seizures. It worked and the seizures stopped. He did have to have a shunt put in to drain the spinal fluid building up where part of the brain was removed. All of this happened right before he came to middle school; no wonder the mom was nervous. She had traveled so far in his journey to have a more normal life. I took careful notes and was sure to work closely with the physical therapist even before Chase came to my class so we would have a solid action plan.

Chase had a sister that was already at our school and was a lovely, kind-hearted girl who adored her brother. All of her friends were really nice to him. In my class, he was such a kind-hearted young man and had polite manners and a fearless spirit. We looked for new ways to complete activities. The occupational therapy and physical therapy departments were great resources. They provided new ways to have him complete tasks. He had such a cheerful and willing attitude and was well-liked by his peers.

When Chase graduated from high school, his mother had a

graduation party for him. The invitation was beautiful and read, "Dear Guests, please know that your whole family is invited to Chase's graduation party. It's a miracle that he is able to walk the stage (as are a lot of special needs children). This carnival-themed party is for all of them with multiple games, toys, and prizes…Please bring your family and if for any reason your child or family can't attend for the reason of transportation, please feel free to call me or email me and we can accommodate you. None of the kids should miss this fun-filled day." This is amazing, I reflected. It was an inclusive celebration of the journey they had traveled. My daughter (who had worked in the occupational therapy department with Chase) and I went to his party, and it was truly an awe-inspiring gala with so many of his friends who had been in my class and their parents attending. We all laughed, played, and took countless pictures in the photo booth. On that day, all the kids were celebrated, and I thanked his mom for understanding the need to celebrate everyone on such an inclusive day of festivities. As I looked around, I was grateful that I had taught many of his peers and was thrilled that he had the tools to lead a successful life.

I would stop and think about his start in life from time to time. He really was a walking miracle. He was successful in high school and had many friends. His sister is now a teacher too and wrote me a lovely letter when she was in college, thanking me for being an inspiration to her. To me, Chase was the inspiration. He has a job and many friends and continues to inspire all those around him.

Tyler

Another student whom I had the privilege to teach, who also went to Chase's high school graduation party, was Tyler. His dad described him as a great guy full of fun and adventure, kindness and grace, love and joy. That is a perfect description, and he was an absolute delight in my classroom. I don't remember him ever getting angry or upset. He didn't know a stranger and would walk up to people with his hand stretched out, saying, "Hi, my name is Tyler." He was adopted at birth and had wonderful, caring parents. Dad was a minister, and mom was a counselor. It was easy to see where his optimism came from, and he was a joy to teach. He loved being in choir, and I could always count on him to learn the correct hand movements and dance steps. He continued to be in choir in high school. It was such fun to watch him as he sang every note and performed every dance move with his choir. He was one of those people that just brought the sunshine with him. In the three years I had him in my class, he made great gains, and the employability skills we started in middle school served him well as he landed his jobs after high school.

Again, my daughter and I got to go to his graduation party. The event was held at his dad's church and was such an incredible jubilee of a high school career that deserved to be celebrated. Making his rounds at each table, Tyler had something nice to say to everyone starting with, "Thank you for coming today." Celebrating this amazing young man that he had grown up to be made me very happy and proud.

After high school, many students chose the additional training afforded to them. Tyler's interpersonal skills were excellent as he was never at a loss for words. This would serve him well as he successfully went through the job training program, strengthening his employability skills along the way. A job at a chain fast food restaurant was a place where he thrived, greeting everyone with his sunny smile and willingness to help.

Tyler works at a wonderful restaurant in town that develops skills and creates jobs for individuals with disabilities. In addition to this job, he works at a clothing store in town. It is wonderful to go to either place and hear the greeting, "Hello, Mrs. Laneville! How are you today?" He always ends the conversation with, "It was good to see you." Be still my heart; those words are music to my ears.

Tony

Chase had many friends, both in my class and in the inclusion classes. A boy named Tony had been friends with Chase since the early days of elementary school. Tony was a boy that found reading very difficult. In the three years I had him, I knew he was a boy that I needed to teach in a more hands-on manner.

Tony loved going to science class and learning how things were made. When it was St. Patrick's Day, he asked me for a box and string and independently made a creative version of what he called "The Leprechaun Trap." He didn't want to show me until it was completed, and I was delighted at his initiative to create this trap. I took pictures of it and showed it to his mom. She replied, "Oh yes, he is always building things around the house."

He continued to love science classes, and instead of having him try to read the material, I would record the book and have him listen to it. He would take his tests orally as well, and he started to soar. When he went to high school, I would talk to him and ask him how it was going. He still took a lot of science classes, and he thrived when he got to work on hands-on projects. The first thing he would always say to me was, "I still love science, Mrs. Laneville." He discovered classes that allowed him to build things and that served him well.

Tony graduated from high school and celebrated that day with Chase. Chase's mom knew the struggles both boys had in school, yet their friendship remained strong, so she told him the party was for him too. That gave him the biggest smile and a day worth celebrating for sure. Today he is gainfully employed at a home and garden store, which is a perfect place for the guy who likes to build things.

Jason

Jason was a boy with a rare syndrome that only about 300 people worldwide have been diagnosed. It is called Cardio-faciocutaneous syndrome, or CFC. I started working with him the summer before he came to middle school and thought that was a wonderful way to get to know him. He loved cooking, and his mom did a great job of promoting his skills in the kitchen. Every year his parents would host a chili cook-off to provide funds for research for this rare syndrome.

They were great advocates for Jason and taught me much about finding new ways to help students succeed. Every time he made a transition to a new school, from elementary school to middle school, to high school, he would develop a crush on one of the ladies. In elementary school, it was his teacher. In middle school, it was one of my aides, and then again, in high school, it was another aide. He was very thoughtful and would write letters, send pictures, and even suggest fashion choices for that person. He learned to text people and use lots of emojis to make his point. These were ways to strengthen his skills and help him form relationships. It made me happy to see the creative ways he would express himself.

Molly

Molly was a gregarious and cheerful girl with Down syndrome. Her mom and her elementary teacher had warned me that I needed a firm hand with her and that she would take advantage of the situation whenever possible to get her way. I valued this information, so the first time she told me she was not going to PE class, I firmly said, "Oh yes, you are going. This is not a choice." She looked at me, gave me a salute, and said, "Yes sir!" I learned that whenever she said that, she was taking you seriously. Her stepdad was in the military, and she respected him. It was funny to hope for, but I was always happy when she would give me that affirmative "Yes sir!", so I knew she would comply. From Molly, I learned that some children need very specific directives spoken with a firm voice. This did not mean yelling or even raising your voice, but the tone needed to be firm with no pause for discussion.

One day Molly was in her physical education class with her aide, who sweetly said, "Molly would you like to come into the dressing room now to change into your street clothes?" Molly seized on the opportunity to run to the hall, for in her mind, she saw it as a choice, and she would rather see who was in the hall during that time. When I found her in another classroom, I asked Molly what she was doing. Molly looked at me and said, "Well, she asked me if I would like to come, and I didn't want to, so I went to visit Mrs. Harris' class."

I remembered the lesson I had learned in my first years of teaching. Everyone needs to be on the same page when working with a child with special needs, and consistency is the key. I explained to her aide that she needed to be firm and never start a sentence with "Would you like to" when addressing Molly because the answer would be no in most situations. Molly needed to understand her boundaries, and chaos would ensue when she was not given those boundaries. Once everyone working with her understood that concept, she was a much easier girl to work with and became quite a delight.

Adrian

Adrian was a boy in a wheelchair who used a communication device to talk. Cerebral palsy made movement very difficult for him, and he needed help with a lot of self-care needs. His hands and legs were both in braces, and he could effectively use one of his hands. The summer before he came to my class, I went to his house and began to learn how to talk to him, help with his self-care, and help him have a successful start to middle school. His mother and the therapists were all very helpful and patient with me. I had never had a student who did not talk, and I was a little intimidated by the whole setup since technology had never been my strong suit.

Both academic tasks and fun things like books on tape and jokes were programmed on Adrian's device. My job was to help him utilize this device to express his wants and needs. When the school year began, I felt much more confident that I could help him succeed in school. I started to realize how much someone could say without saying a word. Adrian's eyes told his mood, and even the slightest movement of his head had meaning. Student tutors would come in and help him. He would not only work on communicating and using his device but also independently navigating his wheelchair through the halls with the use of buttons.

Adrian would flirt with the pretty girls, smiling and going to the joke page when they would try to help him. It made me laugh on the inside when I told this charmer it was not joke time, but work time. I instructed the girls to be firm with him and warned them what a charmer he could be. It was a privilege to help him among the regular education students, and the guidance counselor and I hand-picked those students who could receive this honor.

To practice awareness of all abilities, Adrian went to each home base with me in our school, and I talked about how people can say so much without using their voice. He used his communication device to tell jokes to the students, and we answered some very thoughtful questions after each talk. Adrian helped me bring awareness to our school. Students had to have good grades, be mature and make good use of their time to be able to tutor him. He loved the attention, and the other students loved the status of being able to tutor Adrian. It was definitely a situation where everyone benefitted.

Adrian was in my class for three years. I felt I had been given a gift of knowledge. It amazed me how much a person who could not speak with his mouth could talk and communicate with the rest of the world. I learned so much about communication from my time with him. Everyone in the school learned the value of listening to the voice of other people, even when they are not physically able to talk.

For eighth-grade graduation, it is a tradition in our school to shake the hands of all the eighth-grade teachers in an ending ceremony on the last day. I pushed Adrian's chair and helped him shake other teachers' hands. As he did, there were tears of immense pride in my eyes at how far he had come and how much he had taught me in the world without words. If you pay attention, a shift of the eyes, a raised eyebrow, or a blink can sometimes say more than words.

Miracle League

In my town, we have this wonderful summer baseball league called "The Miracle League." Deserving of this name, there are children of all exceptionalities in this league. It doesn't matter that a person is blind, in a wheelchair, cannot hold a bat independently, or uses crutches to walk. All players that need help are assigned a buddy, and that buddy helps the player do whatever is necessary to go to bat and run the bases. It is an amazing event to watch. I first started just watching the games and later became a baseball buddy. I knew that the purpose of making baseball accessible to everyone was an idea I could embrace.

This was an amazing experience for me, and my job was to protect the player, either in the outfield or when at bat. Sometimes I would have to help keep the player focused to bat the ball, to try again, to run for the ball, to throw it to someone else, or whatever else was needed to help them play the game. I would always come away thinking that there could be a movie made about each game, for so many good things happened in the course of the game. All players get up to bat, and they keep batting until they make a hit. It was a community gathering rather than a baseball game, and everyone was accepted at that person's skill level.

If a baseball tee is needed to help the batter hit the ball, it is put in place. If assistance is needed to hold the bat, or tell the batter where the ball is coming, that assistance is given. The players in the outfield all are in position, ready to make the big play. The score is not kept so that at the end of the game, everyone's a winner. Everyone from each side cheers the batter.

Sometimes, the batter is cheered because he made it around the bases with his leg braces and only fell down once. Sometimes, the player is cheered on because he has the focus to hit the ball independently for the first time. The crowd goes wild, and everyone cheers. People on the field give the batter a high-five as he/she rounds the bases. It is truly heartwarming to witness. With an artificial turf surface that is friendly to wheelchairs and bouncing baseballs, this league provides great opportunities for individuals with mental and/or physical challenges to play the great game of baseball.

Donte was on the team, and he would go through this whole ritual of movements dedicated to his favorite baseball player, Sammy Sosa. I think it involved a kiss, pat, kiss, pat, peace sign, and then the sign of the cross. He would then point to an area beyond the fence line as if to tell you that is how far the ball would go. It was the same ritual every time he was at bat. You could see the sheer joy in his eyes as he took his turn at bat. He was his own cheering section, chanting merrily as he ran around the bases. As the years went on, each child grew in confidence and felt celebrated. A fully accessible playground provided a welcome retreat before and after games were played.

One of the first students I helped was Tim. Since Tim lived with his grandma, who didn't have the stamina to run with him, I felt I could be his helper and provide the opportunity for him to be involved in an organized sport. Our team included a girl who is legally blind, a few kids with autism, a couple kids with Down syndrome and a couple with cerebral palsy. There are five teams in the league, and I go away from each game marveling at the sportsmanship, effort and team spirit on all these teams. The players, the buddies, the crowd and the parent helpers all have two goals in mind, and that is to make everyone feel like a winner and be safe. In my mind, the games are played as I think all games should be played. This is good sportsmanship at its best.

One game, I was helping Tim at bat, telling him to run to first base after his hit. He was running fast and straight for the base. The guy at first base had his own personal baseball in his hand. He stepped on the base and shouted, "You're out!" Tim looked surprised since this had never happened. The first baseman's eyes twinkled, and he started laughing. "Just kidding!" he said, with a huge grin on his face. Tim laughed too, and this was a great play since Tim previously had a hard time knowing when someone was teasing or not.

Every summer, I marveled at the resilience of these amazing students and still think a movie should be made celebrating each and every one of them. There are so many moments to celebrate. Every child had a song playing over a loudspeaker when he or she first got up to bat. This song was personalized for that child. Sometimes this would result in a spontaneous dance party, both on and off the field. No matter how many times it took, the batter tried until they finally got a hit. At the end of the game, the two teams shook hands, telling each other, "Good game"; then they got a snack and a juice box. A person can't help but feel joy in the moment. This was a celebration, and every person walked away feeling like a winner. I continue to volunteer as a Miracle League helper for other students who need assistance.

Summer School

I would try to take some sort of continuing education each summer. When I had the opportunity to take a class that came with free hands-on learning kits from a local university, I jumped at the chance. It was a class that talked about the different types of intelligence and how sometimes students with learning difficulties were great hands-on learners. The theme was an invention fair, and at the beginning of the school year, I put these skills to work. The science teacher had taken the class with me, and I had two students that were struggling readers. They had little interest in lectures but were enthusiastic when told to make and build. They got to make a race car in science using the kits that I had obtained.

They immediately got to work and created an excellent model. Their cooperation and hard work paid off, and they won a ribbon at the fair. This bolstered their self-esteem, and one of the boys continued to thrive and learn with many hands-on learning opportunities. This taught me to look for different ways to teach my learners and realize there are many different types of intelligence.

Austin

Years later, I saw one of my former students at the place I got my hair cut. Austin introduced me to his wife and daughter, and then he said, "This was the teacher that showed me I was smart. I still use that math you taught me." Austin owns his own landscape company, which is a marvelous way for a hands-on learner to earn a living. I told him how proud I was of him and felt pride for the recognition of having helped him. He could have become a behavior problem and dropped out of school, but because we both realized he was a hands-on learner, Austin became a successful and contributing member of our town.

Marie

Marie was a girl in a wheelchair and was defined as medically fragile. She was born with a rare chromosome disorder that left her non-verbal and has a misshapen spine. She joined the class as a new student, and once again, I was unsure how I would be able to communicate with her. I found out she loved music, and she loved movement.

Every day I would tell her how cute her shoes were, because she was quite the fashionista. I wore a pair of sparkly silver shoes like hers and pointed them out to her. We would play happy tunes when she was in the room, and I would grab the wheelchair and dance with her.

Her laugh brought an instant smile to my face. This must be what the voice of an angel sounds like. She could easily tell us what she liked and did not like. She pushed away things that were not of interest, examined items of interest, and if they were really pleasing, she laughed. It brought an instant sense of happiness to the room.

When it was time for lunch, we would give Marie a choice of different flavors of yogurt, and she would pick the one she wanted. It continues to amaze me to this day how a person can communicate without saying a single word. She would look at the person helping and smile. Sometimes she would take her hand and sneakily knock off the yogurt she did not like, then smile sweetly.

To get Marie to laugh, I would step up on the table to try to insert a video into the video machine. The machine was mounted from the ceiling, so to get to it, I would have to step up on the table to put the video in the machine. She would just stare at me and give me the most incredulous look as if to say, "Are you nuts! What are you doing?" After a moment, the most joyous belly laugh would come out of her tiny body, and she just shook with happiness. Sometimes I would just randomly stand on a chair just to get a reaction from her. Another thing she thought was hilarious was I would put a Kleenex box on the tray of her wheelchair. Her little finger would inch forward from her hand, and she would knock it off her tray. She would then look at me laughing, and we would repeat this "game" until it was time to work.

Marie, too was involved in Miracle League and loved the opportunity to be with her peers. She had a peer helper at bat and ran her wheelchair around the bases. Marie's nonstop grin told the story of a happy girl playing baseball with her friends. She taught me many lessons. By careful observation, I learned what she liked, what she didn't like, and what made her respond with a wonderful belly laugh that was music to my ears.

JJ

JJ was a boy in a wheelchair whom I referred to as Mr. Inquisitive. He wanted to know everyone's birthdays, including all the adults, and even our family members. He was very interested in everyone's life. He could tell me not only when my birthday was but my daughter's as well, and he genuinely cared about other people. He had muscular dystrophy and always had an upbeat, happy personality. He loved to talk to the adults and had a great memory for details. Because he was in a wheelchair and had no mobility other than his arms, he needed changing in our back room. Because he was a very aware middle school boy, we would try to preserve his dignity as much as possible. It could have been very awkward, but JJ helped out by telling knock-knock jokes to break the tension. Because of his size, it was a 2-person job with the assistance of an electric body transfer lift. He was always so appreciative of our help and attendance to his needs, and we appreciated his great outlook on life. His attention to detail and remembering everyone's birthday brought joy to everyone in the class.

Jennifer

This girl was another ray of sunshine with a personality to match. She loved to be a helper in the room and had quite the funny sense of humor. She was happiest when she was doing her work, even though some of it was very hard for her. The birth complications made some parts of learning very challenging.

Jennifer would try every task and never give up. As a reward, we had dance parties in my room with chocolate for those who accomplished their goals for the day. She was driven to work hard, so she always got her chocolate. She thought it was hilarious to tell me we eat chocolate, have dance parties, and then work. She would even tell other people that, including the Human Resource Director of our school district. Great, I thought, just how I want to be viewed. Fortunately, he knew her very well and knew the work we did in my class, so he knew she was kidding.

Her social skills were better than most people who are neurotypical or in regular classrooms. When we would sit around the kidney-shaped table and practice saying things like giving each person compliments for something about his or her behavior, she could always be counted on for coming up with genuine and kind things to say. This came so easily to her and was second nature. Writing notes of encouragement and support continues to this day, and she is quick to celebrate friends' achievements or to tell the adults in her life that she was thinking of them. She always remembered people's names and was always delighted to see people she had known from other situations. If I had a substitute aide in my class, Jennifer would be the first to greet them, remembering not only their names but their children's names. She was such a good greeter that she got to be a helper in our front office with our school secretaries. That was an excellent job for her, and she proved once again to be my Goodwill Ambassador. I believe that is her calling in life.

I created an event called Spring Fling Dessert Luncheon as a way to teach my students practical life skills, social skills, and how to host a party. It was also a way to show appreciation to the staff in support and acceptance of my students. This was always held on the Friday right before spring break, celebrating the victories of the first three quarters of hard work for everyone. Beginning several weeks before, we would start making desserts in class that could be frozen. We picked out recipes that we could make as a group. One of our favorites was a chocolate sandwich cookie, whip cream, and pudding dessert I called Kansas Dirt Cake because my family lived in Kansas when I first made it. The other one was strawberry pretzel salad, and my students enjoyed crushing the pretzels to make the bottom layer. We called them our signature dishes, and students had much pride in making them.

Valuable skills, such as reading a recipe, measuring the ingredients accurately, and following the steps of a recipe, were practiced for this event. Kitchen safety, cooperation, cleaning, and organizing our classroom were all part of the hard work that went into the preparation for this event. We made invitations for the event that were hand delivered by the students, and bulletin boards thanking the staff showed our appreciation. We talked about how this was our way to thank the staff and practiced giving compliments that we would use on the day of the Spring Fling. The simple "please and thank you" good manners were stressed.

Every student was assigned a task the day of the event, including greeter, server, bus person, drink refill person, and clean-up crew. The students made labels for all the food, placed tablecloths and flowers on the tables, and played beautiful music, adding to the atmosphere. Teachers were invited during their lunchtime to come to our classroom to enjoy all the goodies we made. When we had our Spring Fling Dessert Luncheon for the staff, it was Jennifer who hosted the event, saying, "Welcome to Room 109. We are so happy you are here."

When other students had success, Jennifer was the first to congratulate them. To this day, she sometimes calls me and asks me if we are having a dance party in my class. There haven't been students who loved it as much as she did, so the answer is usually no. She then says, "Remember, it is chocolate, dance parties, then work," knowing very well that was not the way things worked. The true saying was work, maybe chocolate, and maybe dance parties. She loved to tease me in that way and told me that when I retired, she would take my place.

She still checks in with me, asking me how my weekend or day went. Jennifer then shares the trials and tribulations of her day. She currently works in a T-shirt shop in town, and I am sure people come in just to see her. She still likes to remind me that we ate chocolate, had dance parties, and then did work. I remind her she has the order wrong, and we both laugh. If the world had more people like Jennifer, it would be a happier, more inclusive place. Jennifer continues to be a Goodwill Ambassador in life, and I feel blessed that I was her teacher.

Peter

Peter was a boy in my room who was once labeled

"oppositional defiant." He had Down syndrome and was difficult to understand. He loved to wear all sorts of neckties, so I stocked up on as many fun, patterned ties as I could find. I got seasonal ones for every occasion and all kinds of wild colors, for I knew he liked bright colors.

A behavior specialist observed him a couple of years ago and said he needed to be on a behavior plan. When I got him in my class, this did not faze me, for I felt like I had a lot of tools in my behavior toolbox. I created a behavior program for him with lots of choices and opportunities for success. The behavior program also had lots of positive rewards combined with clear-cut consequences.

Peter had attended school with another classmate named Georgia since kindergarten. She was a sweet girl with Down syndrome who was very cooperative and sometimes could get Peter to do whatever I asked him to do. I learned that for many students with Down syndrome, success was all about relationships. These two had a wonderful relationship. It was important for me to celebrate that and use it as a tool in my classroom. They were a sweet pair, and I welcomed her calming nature and effect on Peter. Georgia loved to mother him, and Peter allowed her to tell him what to do.

Peter's mom began having an increasingly difficult time getting him to come to school. I threatened to come to Peter's house to get him up and out of bed. I had his mom's permission to do this, so I called her up on a difficult day and asked if I could try to get him to school. She said yes, so an aide and I went to his house, knocked on the door, and Mom let us in. The aide I took was a no-nonsense, you better shape up quickly type of person that was perfect for the task. She had been with me since the beginning of my time at this school, and we could finish each other's sentences when it came to our students. We stood in the foyer as his mom yelled up to him in his bedroom and said, "Mrs. Laneville is here, and she is going to get you out of bed to get you to school!" That shocked him, so he quickly got ready, came down the stairs and willingly went on the bus. Mom laughed and said, "I have never seen him move so fast in his life!" I guess the thought of your teacher getting you out of bed to go to school is a great motivator. Sometimes, you just have to make a believer out of them, and that day, I know we accomplished that task. Peter was able to get to school on time for the rest of his middle school days.

The best way to describe Peter is that on certain days if I say the sun is shining, he will tell me it is cloudy, or if I say the crayon is black, he will say it is white. Most days, the behavior program worked. However, one day nothing was working. He would not go up to his next-period class. He refused to cooperate, so he quickly went through the rewards and consequences program. I was out of all the tools I usually use in my behavior toolbox.

One thing I know about him is that he is deeply religious. He loves to go to church on Sundays, and he loves to sing church hymns. Every Monday, he wrote in his journal that going to church was the highlight of his weekend. He is a Roman Catholic and tries to sneak his crucifix into his desk so that he can pretend he is a Priest. I had the aides start singing "Hallelujah" and told him to go up the stairs with them and he could sing too. It worked. He happily went up the stairs. There is a place that sounds like an echo chamber between the first and second story of the school, so he starts singing, "Hallelujah!" He had a beautiful, deep singing voice with vibrato, Divine Intervention. His mother told me that he has a church set up in a room at home. He pretends he is the Priest saying mass. She said that he put various chairs from around the house in rows and had a table in the front of the room. God must be smiling at the little angel with a crooked halo.

For twelve years, I was co-director with one of my aides for the school plays. She needed someone to help her, and since I had been in plays in high school and college, I thought it was something I could do. I always looked for ways to include my students, whether it be giving them a part in the play, having them help build the set or working on costumes, or handing out programs the day of the performance. It was a great new way for us to be inclusive, blending my love of drama with my love of special education. We tried our hand at directing musicals, and this time my co-director was the music teacher. We continued to include my students whenever possible.

As the drama director, it was my job to tidy up the costume department from time to time. A few years prior, we put on a play that had swashbuckling musketeers and also had beautiful costumes, thanks to my good friend Ann. The musketeer's robe was a beautiful royal blue with a silver lame' cross on the front. To the rest of the world, this looked like the cloak of a noble musketeer. To Peter, the minute he put it on, he gasped, as if given a rare gem, and made the sign of the cross, then said, "Jesus Christ, Amen." In his mind, he was now a Priest. I gave him the cloak, and his mother tells me it is now at a place of honor in his "church." It just goes to show you that imagination is not limited to the world of the average child.

Peter had a grooming and hygiene goal that included brushing his teeth at school. He had been shown the proper way to do this activity and was going into the class bathroom to brush his teeth. This was a daily ritual, and I felt like he was making good progress. One day the speech teacher came out of the bathroom with the handheld urinal we used for one of the boys in a wheelchair that was a member of my class. She asked the very disturbing question, "Why is there toothpaste on this?" We all shuddered. We knew the truth. Poor Peter thought it was a rinsing glass. Yes, we always sanitized it after usage, but still, the thought was very disturbing to all of us. I quickly told him that he could not use that for rinsing his mouth, gave him the little Dixie cups to use, and watched him practice rinsing with those. I told his mother what happened, and I am happy to report he was fine, suffered no ill effects, and that she had a good sense of humor.

Peter sees the world differently than most people. There is joy in little things, and he loves things at the most elemental level. I recently saw his mother at the grocery store, and she told me a story about Peter that supports this idea. One weekend he went with his brother and mother to Columbus, Ohio, to attend a trading card show. Mom is a widow and his older brother is in high school. It is a tough job to raise two sons by herself. She works hard to meet the needs of two very different sons. The son in high school collects cards and is interested in attending this trade show. She and Peter were mainly along for the ride and had to find ways to entertain themselves, as the trade show held no interest for Peter. There was a parade going on that day that was a Gay and Lesbian Pride parade. She and Peter watched it, and he was delighted at all the rainbow colors and colorful costumes. Peter thought it was wonderful. Rainbow umbrellas were twirled, and Peter gave his sign for applause and happiness as the people marched past them. To him, it did not mean anything other than people marching in a parade. It was a great day, and he was excited to see all the colorful costumes. What a wonderful outlook on life. If we all could see the world in terms of colors and costumes, maybe the walls of prejudice would come down. His mother said, "I understand why God gave me Peter. He sees things at their most elemental level." It is this understanding of life and complete innocence that gives her pause to appreciate life herself. When they got home, Peter was delighted to find that she, too, had an umbrella with colors, so he opened it and twirled it, remembering all the sights and sounds of the day.

September 11, 2001

On September 11, 2001, a tragedy struck our nation that left my students in pieces. What I have learned teaching special education for many years is that when a national disaster happens, students tend to personalize it. They wonder what effect it has on their lives. They wonder if their loved ones will be impacted. There were four coordinated terrorist attacks by the militant Islamic terrorist group al-Qaeda against the United States. Although we did not watch it on TV at school, students certainly saw it at home on their televisions. They heard their parents talk about it and heard others discuss it. Once again, I was uncertain how to help them understand this horrific news, but I knew I needed to refocus my students. We read stories about the heroes of that day. I went back to my discussion about how when something bad happens, always look for the helpers. I listened to their concerns. I tried to give them facts without fear and reassure them that they were okay. The phrase, "Look for the "helpers," became my mantra whenever something bad happened. That day I gave extra hugs, listened extra hard, and tried to calm the fears in my students.

My youngest daughter was in eighth grade at the time, and usually, we did not see each other much during the day. However, on that devastating day, she came to my room with a girlfriend. They both had such sad looks on their faces. She simply said, "I just need a mom hug." I hugged her for a long time, then hugged her friend as well. The friend responded, "Thank you, Mrs. Laneville. I needed that."

DuWayne

One boy in my class loved anything to do with lawn care. His name was DuWayne, and he was very well-behaved. He said he would have a lawn care business when he grew up, so we focused his reading on the responsibilities of having your own company, working with plants, and anything I could link to this type of career. DuWayne loved to mow lawns and was a great rule follower and a people pleaser.

One time he made me really laugh. I got a perm in my hair and returned to school with curly hair. DuWayne looked at me and said, "Let me guess, is it a crazy hair day?" I laughed and said, "No, it is not. I got a perm in my hair because I wanted something different." He quickly responded, "Well, that was going to be my next guess!" We had a good laugh about that one and his quick comeback. As an adult, DuWayne has his own lawn care business and has added snow shoveling in the winter.

Dani

When Dani began as a new student, we didn't even realize she was the new girl we were getting. I knew I had a new student arriving that day, but she looked like a grown-up and carried herself so that she could pass for a staff member. When I was introduced to her, I thought, "Will this be a help or a hindrance that she looks like an adult?"

I soon found out that it was a help, and she clearly was very comfortable talking to adults, spending most of her time around adults. She lived with her mom, and Mom expressed interest in getting Dani some girlfriends her age. Things went very well with Dani as she was a good and cooperative student. She really saw herself as an adult and had difficulty relating to girls her age. I decided to use some typical peers and girls in my class who had good social skills to model for Dani what it looked like to have conversations with girls her own age. She loved music and found joy in talking to another girl about music. They both liked a boy band and talked about attending a concert. This small group of girls talking to each other tremendously strengthened her conversation skills. The other girls in my class saw her as a new friend. Even though Dani was only in my room for a year, I felt like we had given her the tools to form new friendships with girls her own age.

Mitch

I taught a higher-level reading class for a few years with another teacher. It was a program that targeted and addressed specific reading needs with assessment at regular intervals on targeted skills. This helped students and teachers analyze and track performance. The program had three parts: independent reading, small group instruction, and computer work that targeted comprehension, writing, and vocabulary building. Mitch loved the structure of this class, as he always knew what the day would bring. He was a sweet and compliant student who had an amazing memory. As a student with autism, his superpower was that he could immediately recite the release year of popular children's movies when asked. An internet search on my part always proved him right. Sometimes he would ask me, "Do you want the first time it came out or the re-release date?" He loved to joke around and loved sarcasm. As a higher-functioning student, he continued to thrive in school. I loved that he wanted to be in the plays that I directed with my friend while he was in middle school. His powerful memory would serve him well as he continued to audition and get parts in community theater productions.

Asher

Asher was another boy with autism that was really fun to meet. He had a wonderful imagination and was very creative. In eighth grade, a parent/staff meeting occurred, and Asher returned to public school after a brief trial of private and home-schooling. He had a funny sense of humor. He participated in the school play, which featured Zombies. In one scene during practice, the prop we used was a stick with a glove on the end to create an illusion of a hand moving in midair. Asher thought changing the life-sized hand with a doll-sized hand would be hilarious, so he did it without telling anyone. I decided to keep it in the play.

Even though I did not teach any of Asher's classes, my aides were in regular classes to help him. My class was kind of a safety net for him; if he ever got overwhelmed and needed a break, he could come to my class. He would use my computers as a free time activity. He would tell me about the cool things they were learning in eighth-grade science, one of his favorite classes.

Sometimes he would talk to me in his cartoon voice and laugh. He was a people person and had a great connection with his science teacher, always wanting to share a joke with him. As a reward, he loved to watch animation videos. He loved stop-motion animation, like the effect you get when you make flip books where the characters appear to move. It is an animated filmmaking technique in which objects are physically manipulated in small increments between individually photographed frames to appear to exhibit independent motion. He would also use this as a reward when he had occupational therapy support.

Asher hated to write anything down, but in keeping with his sense of humor, he would say, "I am going to only use these world's best pencils because that is what they are advertised to be." Asher always thought he was funny when he said that line. He had a great sense of humor, loved to tell jokes, and was always pleasant, brimming with new ideas. He first worked on handwriting but later learned to do voice-to-text, as he was very good with technology. He played trombone in the band, and to help keep him focused, he had an aide who enjoyed his great sense of humor. When he did marching band in high school, it was fun to watch his concentration, and he continued to thrive in the band community.

Asher's parents were wonderfully supportive and celebrated all his unique gifts, encouraging him to find more theater opportunities. He joined a community theater group with the help of his parents. Here, Asher's star shines brightly. His creativity, enthusiasm, and ability to do different voices continue, and he keeps finding other ways to entertain.

<u>Mitch and Asher go to college!</u>
Kent State University in Kent, Ohio, has a brilliant Career and Community Studies program. The non-degree transitional program prepares students with intellectual and developmental disabilities through academic pursuits, peer socialization, and career discovery. This program maximizes opportunities to prepare these students to become self-determined adults. It creates meaningful experiences for these young adults. Students must be at least 18 and have completed high school graduation requirements. This was the perfect place for two former students, Mitch and Asher, to thrive.

Mitch and Asher are currently sharing a dorm room as roommates. I am so proud of them, as I know they both have excellent social skills and gifts to share with the world. Mitch and Asher are hardworking students and have held jobs before this program. Mitch stated that he did not feel fulfilled in his position, so he was in the program to learn and grow. Wow! What an honest and mature outlook on life. I know these young adults will continue to thrive and be valuable contributing members of society.

Valerie

Valerie was a girl whom I first met in the spring when visiting the elementary school to observe another student I would have in my class in the fall. This was my routine: to watch my incoming students and take as many notes from the elementary teachers' knowledge as possible. They knew these students and knew how to ensure the greatest success with them. Besides what was in the Individual Education Plan, I wanted to know their likes and dislikes. What were some of their favorite things to earn as rewards? What were the things they struggled with in school? I wanted to know how to best create a partnership with the parents.

Another special education teacher was in the hall walking with Valerie, and she said, "Valerie, you can go back to class by yourself." She then said, "I wanted to talk to you about Valerie. I don't know how to describe her, but you will figure it out if you observe her."

I was intrigued and observed her in a typical class with an aide. I noticed Valerie had a lot of anxiety. She would fidget and get upset, then have to leave. I attended her IEP meeting at the end of the year in elementary school. She would benefit from being in my class, which could be considered a safety net.

When Valerie started 6th- grade in my school, I noticed she had an excellent memory and liked to control situations. Her not knowing what was expected of her caused her high anxiety. She wanted a predictable routine, and sixth grade was a new school with a new set of people and situations. She really didn't like constructive criticism, and her anxiety would appear. The first sign I knew she was very anxious was when she would pick at the strings on her clothes. These could be tiny little threads, but by the time she was done, they would become a hole or a ripped seam. If she felt any loose thread, she would work at it until it became a ball of string.

One time we were in my class having the friendship circle. It allowed students to practice social skills and learn social cues. We were all around a kidney-shaped table and were practicing complimenting other people about something they did, i.e., "Jeremy, I like the way you listened quietly to the story." The compliments couldn't be anything about their physical appearance, i.e., "I like your hair, your shirt, your shoes," etc., were unacceptable. The students worked on making eye contact with each person and saying their names. Everyone seemed to be doing a great job, but when it was Valerie's turn, the aide with me said, "Valerie, what is in your mouth? Spit it out, please." It looked like gum, and we had a no-chewing gum policy. Mrs. Johnson held out her hand. "Valerie, please give me whatever is in your mouth now," Mrs. Johnson urged. In hindsight, she probably regretted saying that. Valerie spits out a gigantic ball of string she pulled off her clothes. I thought Mrs. Johnson would lose her breakfast. A massive ball of sopping wet string landed in her hand. That was the first time we noticed two things: Valerie was very clever when pulling strings off her clothes, and these behaviors occurred when she became anxious. Valerie was quite covert, not doing anything to call any attention to herself. Whole seams would unravel on the sides of her shirt, pants, and underwear, and sometimes we needed to call her mom to bring a change of clothes.

Once, Mom and I thought an old sweater from home with many strings would be a good idea, but that quickly fell apart. Valerie became so obsessed that she could not work until it was destroyed. It started as a pretty pink sweater and soon became a giant ball of pink yarn.

Mom was great to work with and was able to bring clothes when we needed them. Mom also had been a teacher, and she was great at trying to problem solve. She would listen in a non-judgmental manner as I explained Valerie's behaviors. We would solve issues together because Mom was aware of her daughter's picking at strings and anxiety. We started using different fidget tools for Valerie to replace the string-picking behavior. We used little squishy balls, anti-stress putty, and other calming tools.

I experimented with different things and found out that I would give her choices since Valerie liked to control the situation. Several times, she would come up to me during the course of a day and say, "Mrs. Laneville, I have a problem." One notable time this occurred, I said, "What is it, Valerie?" "Umm, I kind of don't have underwear," she sheepishly stated. "What! Did you forget to put some on today?" I asked, clearly not understanding what the problem was. "No... yes...well, I did, but I kind of pulled too many strings," she explained. Sure enough, the evidence was in the bathroom. Only a massive pile of strings and shredded cloth remained. A quick phone call to Mom brought the much-needed item. From then on, we kept an extra bag of clothing in her locker.

If something bothered Valerie, she would try to problem-solve the only way she knew how. When she told me she had a string, we immediately cut it to prevent further deterioration.

Valerie needed to know exactly what was happening that day, so I made a schedule for her. We tried to keep that the same, but I would give her advance notice if we needed to change something. She was an intelligent girl and an asset to her regular education classes. Valerie had an excellent memory and memorized essential facts in her regular education classes.

Valerie was allowed to navigate the halls independently between classes, but at times she could be impulsive. An example of this was when she stopped in to say hi to her social studies teacher and another special education teacher who was in his room eating their lunches. Both men liked her and said hi. As the men were talking, Valerie picked up the Intervention Specialist's can of pop and took a drink. "Valerie! Did you just drink my pop?" She sheepishly confessed that, yes, she did indeed drink his pop. Right after that, I came around the corner, and they told me what happened. That afternoon in our friendship circle, we discussed how it is rude and inappropriate to drink someone else's drink.

As she went through middle school, she became more focused on her classes, less anxious, and better able to handle unexpected occurrences during the school day. We conducted our daily friendship circle at the end of the day and discussed different social conventions and situations. Having lots of conversations and role-playing different scenarios helped her realize what was acceptable and what was not. We discussed how to care for our business and refrain from telling others what they should do. It was a skill I thought she had mastered. Although we had practiced saying nice things to others, she couldn't resist correcting another student. Later that afternoon, I found a piece of paper on my desk with directions for knocking someone out by dragging them across a poppy field. She had seen this action in one of her favorite movies. I knew this was her way of telling me she was unhappy with me.

My aides always had a good sense of humor. When the note was found about how to "do me in," they put it on a small dropper bottle to look like some sort of magic potion and placed the bottle in a red fabric bag. It made me laugh, and I kept it with me for the rest of my teaching career. Valerie stopped being mad at me and returned to her same self the next day. I took a picture of the bottle and showed it to her mom, which also made her laugh. To this day, that is one of our inside jokes.

Valerie loved to be in charge of any group activity. When we were once more planning for the Spring Fling Dessert luncheon, I knew what her particular job would be. We practiced sitting at our friendship table and giving compliments, learning to take turns and talk to people kindly.

I usually pick easy-listening music like piano or quiet guitar for the Spring Fling Dessert luncheon. As an 8th grader, Valerie wanted to be in charge of the music. She said she was the DJ and wanted to "crank this party up." She had excellent skills in finding appropriate music, so I knew she could do this task. Her version of cranking it up was listening to popular show tunes. Seeing her take over and be appropriate and focused made me feel she was ready to attend high school and learn some job skills. She had vast moments of social growth with me and tolerance of events that did not fit her scheme. I knew she was ready for high school after that special day of being in charge to "crank this party up."

Valerie returned every spring and helped me run the concession booth of the yearly school musical. We would sit together, and she would watch night after night, memorizing every song and every line. She continues this day to be one of my favorite students to talk to, quickly holding an appropriate conversation that is both insightful and engaging. She has a boyfriend now and can carry on relevant discussions. She can now tolerate different materials, and strings no longer bother her. I am so proud of how far this lovely young lady has come.

Curtis

Curtis joined my room as a 6th grader and was a tall, handsome boy with autism. Curtis loved to watch television and sometimes would have a conversation with me or any other adult at our school. We would think it was a regular conversation but would hear recognizable phrases from a television show. Sometimes he would be at his desk and repeat large portions of a show's dialogue. It was uncanny how these phrases would fit perfectly into the conversation.

I could tell Curtis' brain was wired very differently from mine. It is said that autistic brains show widespread alterations in structure. I wondered how his brain would look if I could see these alterations. I pictured them to be magnificent.

When Curtis became distracted working alone at his desk, you could see his imagination at work. I would tell him to turn off the TV. He would reach for an imaginary button on the side of his neck and say, "Click!" Curtis paused and then returned to his schoolwork. I could always tell when Curtis was not focused on the math program I had assigned on his tablet because this scheming boy's head would tilt. "Curtis! Get back to math", I exclaimed. I knew without even checking that he was playing a warplane video game when his head began to dip and sway, then move side to side. Curtis was fighting an enemy aviator, and I would advise him to get back to work. He was always cooperative, and I rarely had to do more than those few verbal commands.

Things made sense to Curtis when I wrote them down as rules. They became solidly etched in his mind. He was very rule-oriented and would repeat directions to me occasionally, saying things like, "We only use pencils for writing." Once a rule was written down, it became law in his mind, and he never chewed on another pencil again.

Sometimes Curtis would play with me and say silly things like, "No more monkeys jumping on the bed." I would have loved to take a field trip in his brain because the next thing he would say was, "You have to listen to your teachers and your mom." His mom later told me she did say that to him. Those were her words verbatim. I know those were rules in his mind, and maybe the monkeys were just as important as listening to the adults in his life. He was a triplet, and his brother and sister were neurotypical and very supportive of him. Curtis was a fascinating boy, and I enjoyed every minute of being his teacher.

Curtis could know the day of the week for any future date within a 10-year range. It might have been longer than that, but I never tested it out. I could say, "Curtis, what day will it be on November 17th, 2024? "You could pick any date and year, check it, and he would be correct 100% of the time. Certain parts of his brain were in the brilliant savant status, which I found fascinating. At the end of the school year, I saw him on the bus, and he said, "Mrs. Laneville, I was in your room 10 years ago."

Could that be possible? I said, "No, Curtis, it hasn't been ten years." It seemed like only yesterday, but when I thought about it, he was correct, and I was silly to doubt him. Certain things were hardwired into Curtis' brain, and the calendar was one of them.

Oliver

Like Curtis, Oliver was also a tall, handsome boy with autism. He liked to repeat specific references to age-inappropriate movies at the most inappropriate times. I thought those were bizarre things for him to say, as I knew his parents would not let him watch those types of movies. They were lovely people and significantly understood how to help their son. I didn't know that he had an excellent skill set in technology, so Mom explained that he got into his dad's laptop when no one knew he could and found those movies. She apologized, and I told her we would just teach him that those were inappropriate things to say when we were at school. She was mortified that he would say such phrases. I quickly told her he was intelligent and had his own ideas about what he wanted to do, no matter how much good training he had at school or home. He had a knack for waiting until it was quiet reading time, then would shout one of those phrases or wait until they were doing quiet work in his social studies class and shout it out. He then would look around the room.

Oliver knew he would get a lot of attention and could get out of whatever he didn't want to do. The more we objected, the more he would continue to say them. Oliver was very clever in that way, and it took a long time to get him to stop saying those two titles. Another word that he liked to say, out of the clear blue, was "Shiloh"; he would state that one repeatedly, as he liked how it sounded. He said it in a sing-song voice and seemed to be chanting. It seemed soothing to him, but as the pitch got higher and the volume louder, it was not pleasing to anyone else. We had read "Shiloh" in class, and Oliver seemed to enjoy saying the title. It became almost a soothing mantra to him, so he was allowed to use that as long as he wasn't disturbing anyone else.

Carter

Carter was a boy who had four different types of seizures. We discovered these were focal, generalized, a combination of focal and generalized, and unknown. In layman's terms, it meant he had a lot of different types of seizures. Any of them could be a sudden, uncontrolled electrical disturbance in his brain that we would have to know about and take action. We received training from our medical team at school. We carefully read his records, as well as a notebook that the previous school had created. His mother and a former teacher provided valuable information. They both talked about the notebook that was like a diary of his school day. I was happy when the teacher gave me the notebook, as it would give me clues as to what to expect and how she handled the different seizures.

When we heard that he was coming to our class, we quickly assembled a team of first responders to be prepared for him. We reviewed the basic comfort care of first aid and how to keep someone calm and comfortable, away from imminent dangers. We discovered that he would lose consciousness and have violent muscle contractions for three minutes when he had a grand mal seizure. We needed to start a timer and administer rectal diazepam when these grand mal seizures occurred. This involved turning Carter on his side, facing one of the care team first responders, and bending his upper leg forward. The syringe tip would be gently inserted into his rectum until the rim was snug against the rectal opening. A slow count to 3 while pushing in the plunger until it stopped was the last step.

We had to be trained for this protocol and devise a plan to preserve his privacy if it happened in the classroom. The team practiced many scenarios and developed various procedures until we were ready to tackle this daunting task. I was given a communication device to have quick access to the school nurse and front desk secretaries, who could then alert the rest of the team. We knew that if the seizure lasted more than 5 minutes, we needed to call 911. Fortunately, we never had to go to that step with Carter, but we were prepared to take the necessary action.

The day arrived when Carter came to my class. We felt like we were prepared for the medical aspects of his life, but we did not really know what Carter's personality was like. Even though he did not speak, he saw everything that went on in the class and was often amused by the antics of other students. He did not miss any shenanigans, and his eyes would light up when he saw the mischief caused by other students. He was very stubborn; he wouldn't look at the adult trying to help him if he didn't want to do the work.

For the first few weeks, we exclusively kept him in my class. A peer helper liked to come to my class to help my students. She was a beautiful, gregarious person, and Carter's face would light up the minute she went into the room. We soon realized he could do more challenging work, and I felt he was ready to try a few classes outside my room. The science teacher was very engaging and always had hands-on lessons. Often, students would work in groups. We added Carter to the other two students in that class with two aides and watched as he became captivated by the lessons. Soon, it became time for the trio to present to the class. The presentation was a slideshow with pictures and words. The subject was different types of sharks. They had worked hard on this project and created terrific slides detailing the different types of sharks. Carter's job was to hold the posters the three of them had made. It was all going well until they lost their focus.

First, one of the boys discovered that you could make shadow puppets with the light from the slideshow, so that became his focus. Bunnies and alligators danced across the screen. This caused just a couple of chuckles from the audience. This caused the second boy to start saying names of horror movies. It was like a chain reaction had been set into motion. He suddenly tried to grab the crotch of his aide, who quickly moved away. The good thing was that all three were behind a tall lab table, so no other students would witness that spectacle. We had yet to learn what prompted that. She could have gotten an Academy Award because her face remained impassive and didn't miss a beat, then quickly moved away. He got back on task. The first boy quit making shadow puppets after the other aide gave him "the look." All the while that was happening, Carter was grinning from ear to ear, thinking the whole thing was hilarious.

Thanks to the aide's quick thinking, the slideshow ended, and the focus was on the poster that Carter was holding. Finally, the presentation was over. It felt like an epic fail, yet amazingly, the rest of the students just acted like nothing out of the ordinary had happened. They did not witness much of the shenanigans behind that lab table. When the presenters sat down, everyone gave them a resounding round of applause, and Carter grinned.

When we returned to the classroom, we discussed properly giving a presentation. There was still a smirk on Carter's face, for he remembered how entertained he was when their presentation was contrary to how it should have been presented. During a class presentation, we discussed personal boundaries, focus, and saying appropriate things. As the aide prepared his food in the blender for lunch, he continued to have a big smirk for the rest of the day. Thankfully, he did not have any seizures that day.

Byron

Byron was a boy that I knew had a tough home life. His parents were divorced in a contentious split, both trying to get custody of Byron. He lived with his mom. Knowing that I tried to gather as much information from his elementary teacher as possible to help this boy transition to middle school. He had more disruptive and violent behaviors at home than at school. I knew I needed to make sure school was always a safe and predictable place for him.

Byron's elementary teacher had terrific insights, and she described the many challenges he faced every day. She significantly understood his wants and needs since he was a non-verbal boy with autism. He had many sensory needs and many behaviors to address. I observed him several times as a fifth-grade student, and she gave me a detailed list of how to meet those needs when I visited her class. I talked to his aide, who understood what rewards he would work for, what things could trigger an outburst, and how to get him settled back down if he should lose control. They told me the books he wanted the teacher or aide to read to him and gave me one of his favorites. Our school system required us to take CPI or Crisis Prevention Intervention, and I paid close attention to how to meet his needs.

In sixth grade, he made the transition very well when he came to middle school. He had a set routine and a one-on-one aide who was very patient and calm. He loved to have stories read to him, and she did a great job reading in a soothing voice.

Even though he was non-verbal, he told us his wants and needs by pointing to things. We read to him as a reward after he finished his work. One of the books I read was one his elementary teacher told me he liked. It was "Brown Bear Brown Bear," and I read it using different voices as she had done. It always made him laugh. The aide read him a book with the word "mama" in it, which was the one word he could say, and as she got to that word in the book, he would say it. I thought we were on a great path and had smoothly transitioned to middle school. He liked to tease us by hiding things around the room. Sometimes it was the remote control, and he would laugh as we would look amongst the books on our bookshelf. We always found the 'missing" object, and he delighted in playing this little game.

We thought things would go smoothly the following year, but things changed in seventh grade. Nothing that had previously worked was working. It was typical around seventh grade for my students to have hormonal changes, which changed the whole dynamic of their learning in new and unexpected ways. This was combined with changes in his home life which grew even more unstable. It became the perfect storm of disaster, which hit like an earthquake, shaking the dynamics of the whole class. That combination is so tough to navigate. When kids with special needs have changes in their bodies at the middle school level, that, in and of itself, becomes a challenge. How could I meet his ever-changing needs and help him remain calm and in control?

When he was in my class, he was in a safe haven filled with schedules, rules, and order. I had no control over what happened at home, and there were changes. He would start his day being agitated. When we would get him ready to go home, he again became very agitated. Yet, I also knew that he would feel safe in a calm, predictable environment while he was with me. For some reason, I thought it was even more critical this year. Still, he started throwing things and becoming a danger to himself and others. He would scream a blood-curdling, siren-sounding scream, which negatively affected the whole class. These screams could last up to 15 seconds. No one was able to perform their tasks at hand. One girl would hide in the bathroom; one boy would cover his ears; and another girl would start crying, visibly shaking, and showing significant signs of distress. The girl who was hiding was shy, to begin with, so when she hid and cried in the bathroom, it broke my heart for her. Byron would try to bite himself and throw things at other students, so I knew having him in the room with others in this state was unsafe. I would have one of the aides take everyone else for a walk because I knew it was vital for them to feel safe too. The stress level of the whole class felt like a volcano about to erupt.

On two separate occasions, Byron grabbed an aide and then me by the hair and yanked so hard we thought we would have a bald spot. This occurred when one of the aides had taken everyone else for a walk. There were only two adults and this distraught boy in the room. We were both trained for such instances, but the training didn't work. It was a humbling experience, and I tried to remain calm even after he finally let go, and my head throbbed.

One day Byron started to scream for no apparent reason, which was a new behavior. It made another student cry, and one hid in the bathroom. His aide came to meet him, and he grabbed her hair at the scalp and yanked it with such force it threw her off balance. We all had been trained to handle situations like this safely for the aggressor and the attacked person. We had been trained to lean into the pull when that happened, but it did not help. Finally, it took three of us to convince him to let go. As time passed, his behaviors grew increasingly violent, throwing books, kicking at walls and doors, and then trying to hit adults. The screaming lasted longer and seemed gut-wrenching and primal, coming from a place deep within his very being. He would hide the books he usually liked us to read. He started throwing his tablet and then screaming. He became unpredictable and more at risk of hurting himself or others. He would try to bite his hand after an incident. It was clear he was losing control. It shook the whole class of students, and everyone felt tense.

I was lucky to have the support of two of my fellow Intervention Specialists, who were brothers and always had a great rapport with students. They were good friends and allies, and I always felt they were willing to help me when necessary. I had the support and empathy of the vice-principal assigned to my students. Together, we decided to have Byron in a room by himself and try to continue instruction from there. This seemed to help briefly, but unacceptable behaviors continued to escalate. He grabbed the laptop from the male teacher's hands and threw it against the wall, leaving a big hole in it. He continued to try to bite himself and punched a hole in the wall. I knew it was time to call in some other experts, for we did not feel we could meet his needs.

Our school psychologist observed him and did a Functional Behavior Assessment. Bryon was given the diagnosis of autism spectrum disorder (ASD), attention deficit/hyper-activity disorder (ADHD), and intermittent explosive disorder (IED). There was no identifiable pattern to the time of day or staff involvement. It could happen at any time with any person. One possible trigger had once been when he was asked to complete non-preferred activities, like academic work, but this no longer holds true. The behaviors and the screaming became more intense and frequent, and the other students continued to hear his outbursts, even across the hall. We had many meetings and finally considered residential treatment programs, or at least had them observe him and offer any suggestions.

After several months of trying to help Byron, many meetings, and observations from behavior specialists, it was determined that the best place for him would be a residential treatment facility. There, Byron could get the 24-hour care he now needed, and it would provide a safe environment for him.

After representatives from two residential programs observed him, they agreed that he would fit in nicely in their programs. It made me feel better when one of the behavior specialists said we were doing a great job with him and acted very professionally. Part of me felt bad because I knew he was going to leave, and we were not going to solve this problem, but part of me knew that this was the best outcome for the whole child. I realized that even though I tried to keep him safe and have a positive environment for him, certain things were beyond my control.

One of the two programs was determined to best meet his needs, and I was happy that he was in a residential program where he could get the total care he needed. He would have a safe, consistent program during the day to meet his academic needs, then have the same consistent program the rest of the day and evening. He thrived there for years. This seemed to be the best outcome for him, and his mental and physical needs could be addressed.

I later found out that he passed away in a hospital. I don't know the details, but it made me very sad. How did he end up in an out-of-state hospital? What was his life like once he left my class? Did he have the stable, caring environment he craved? Did he still hide things and think he was funny when he did it? Did they read to him? He was 19 years old, and seeing his picture in his obituary was disturbing. I understand now that sometimes the most important thing I can do for my students is to make them feel safe and valued and provide them with a predictable, stable, and positive environment. I only get to teach them for a short while, and during that time, I always try to give them the very best, most positive experience that will carry them in life. I don't know the answers to my questions, but I pray that he is finally at peace.

Nate

Many students in my class didn't have any crazy stories that filled my memories but were kind and hard workers in my class. They had supportive families, parents, and grandparents who only wanted the best for their children or grandchildren. Two students that came to mind were Nate and Cordelia.

Nate was raised by his grandparents, as both of his parents were deceased. The grandparents were involved in his education, wanting only the best for him. They held high behavioral expectations for him, and he did not disappoint. He always treated me with the utmost respect. As a boy on the autism spectrum, he was very upfront and honest. He would tell me exactly what he was thinking or how he saw a situation.

I would get many letters of thanks from these wonderful grandparents. They were very supportive of me, and I could tell they read my weekly newsletter. If I said we were low on tissues in the room, they would immediately bring new boxes in. They always told me how much they appreciated my work with their grandson. Grandpa was a minister and helped his community in any way he could. Grandma wanted her grandson to be successful and live a fruitful life. Today, Nate holds two part-time jobs, and I see him in the community from time to time. He lives in an apartment and has a provider who comes to help him from time to time. I love seeing him so successful and know that he was a case of "It takes a village." I was happy to be part of that village.

Cordelia

Cordelia was another student who had such a kind and loving home. Mom shared with me that she had once been in a class of students with special needs. Cordelia and her parents lived with Grandpa and Grandma on her mom's side. Everyone was very supportive of my program, and Mom worked hard to ensure her daughter had great academic successes and bonds of friendship that would carry over as she became an adult. Whether it was a play date with a classmate or a supervised date with a boy, Cordelia had all the family support she needed for success. Cordelia was always a happy girl who worked hard through school. She was another student who really rose to her level of success, surrounded by her village of people. These two students, Nate and Cordelia, had people who loved them, and we all worked together so that they could be positive contributors to society as they became adults.

Bobby

Bobby was a kind-hearted boy who always had a smile on his face. He loved talking to people, and he would first ask if they wanted to see his robot dance. Of course, people would say yes, and he would delight his audiences by doing his impression of a robot to the music in his head. He was very cooperative and responded well to the work assignments. He wasn't particularly concerned with his hair or how he looked, so one day, when I got a request from his mother for a particular "look" for picture day, I was surprised.

Her words are better than mine in this instance, so this is what Bobby's Mother wrote me in an email, "Mrs. Laneville it would not surprise me if you thought I did not groom Bobby's hair for school. Especially in the winter days when he wears and when that hat comes off in the classroom. I can only imagine what a sight he may be with that hair of his. He has no vanity to want to fix it back into a reasonable style and make it look nice…decent maybe…nice...no. So, you said I could contact you about his challenges before the pictures. We really liked the hand in the pocket, serious yet with a smile ear to ear look, without showing braces if possible."

"Wow," I thought. That was a tall order, and not exactly what I meant when I told the parents that picture day was coming and whether we have anyone who was camera shy, etc. I didn't think I had to get one of the students ready to have a certain look.

The note went on to say, "I will send him with a small tube gel. I'd like to give him a (famous actor) look but his hair is so wavy. I know this seems long but just use a tube of gel and comb and I trust you with the rest. BIG BIG smile. No braces if possible. But don't have him struggle not to show. Sorry if this is too much? It's just a hair and teeth thing."

She even included a picture of a heartthrob actor for reference. My first reaction was, is this a joke? But I realized she was serious. That was the strangest picture day request I ever had, and the next year I did not include a note to parents asking if there were any challenges with picture day. Be careful what you ask for is the moral of that story. I tried my best with his hair, and we got a picture that she was happy with, which felt like a victorious accomplishment. I kept the email and read it occasionally, and it now just makes me laugh.

Margaret

Margaret was a girl with Down syndrome who did not like that many other people, nor did she like mornings. She would come to school off the bus in a grumpy mood, and we understood that she didn't want to talk to anyone for a while. That was fine because I understood that not everyone is a morning person. I understood it better when, after many months of trying to engage her to at least make eye contact, she looked at me and threw her shoe at me from across the room. It broke my water bottle, and I received a clear message. Do not engage. This girl does not want to experience my sunny disposition. She had a powerful throwing arm and a deadly aim. She would take off both shoes and lie on the carpet when perturbed with me.

Margaret seemed to connect better with the pets in our room and loved to have free time on her tablet. I tried to include that in her lessons. Progress came slowly, and we finally agreed that if she did her required tasks, she would get to use her tablet for free time. She had a fantastic aide who was patient and many times would wait it out when Margaret refused to look at anyone or do anything. The aide worked hard to show no emotion on her face. I knew Margaret was the captain of her ship and liked to be in control, so I made a choice board showing her that she got choices after completing tasks. I made a home-school behavior chart and instructed her parents to reward her when she finished the required tasks.

I always tried to put myself in the shoes of the parents when I gave them suggestions. I know they always mean well and have their child's best interest at heart, but truth be told, some of my students were very difficult to deal with at home, and sometimes parents needed a break. I understood that this system would take time and probably years of undoing trigger-response reactions to be effective. I did not live daily with their child, but I always admired their constant journey and knew they had their struggles and frustrations. It is always easier just to give in to the behavior, and there is value in self-preservation for the parents. No one is perfect, but these parents were willing to try to use this reward system.

Margaret's parents were lovely people, trying to support me in every effort. Dad made a specially designed bike that she would ride along and be able to pedal while it was hooked to his own bicycle. They had interesting birds and dogs at home, so I knew she loved animals. They would tell me how proficient she was with her tablet, being able to record a movie and capture individual pictures within that movie. She loved to take photos with that tablet at home. Interestingly, when she was at home, she very clearly talked and communicated her wants and needs. At school, she chose not to say a word, and I realized that was one way she could take control of her situation and environment.

One particularly trying day, she entered the restroom with her stuffed animal, Beanie. I'm not sure what Beanie started out to be: a rabbit or dog, maybe, but Beanie looked like a well-loved stuffed animal that traveled many places. Beanie went everywhere with her, and I did not try to change that. I heard the toilet flush and her yelling, "Come back, Beanie!" I heard that loud and clear. I cautiously opened the door, and here was Margaret looking at an empty toilet bowl. I asked her if she flushed Beanie down the toilet, and she nodded, "Yes." It was clear she did not see the connection between cause and effect.

"Did you think Beanie would come back up?" I questioned. "Yes," she simply said. In her mind, Beanie was some kind of magical creature. Beanie would rise from the ashes, or in this case, the toilet bowl. I tried to explain that Beanie was not coming back. She stood there looking at the empty toilet and slowly returned to her seat. I gave her some alone time to process what had just happened. Maybe that day, she learned the critical lesson that actions have consequences. Later that week, another Beanie came to take its place. Dad had figured out how to recreate Beanie, so he made a new one for her. We called it Beanie 2.0. Through the years, various forms of Beanie would appear. Last summer, when I helped with her

Miracle League team, I noticed she only had "Beanie Head." I am unsure how that story will continue, but I know that she has great parents who only want the best for their daughter.

Fab Five

The following year, five new sixth graders came into my class whom I liked to call "The Fab Five." None of them had significant behavioral issues, and they all loved attending their regular 6th-grade science class. Because there were five students, one with Down syndrome, two with autism, and two with cognitive difficulties, an aide and I were in this class to support them. The regular education teacher said he liked having my kids in his classroom. I knew that was a true statement. He was entertaining, engaging, and accepting, which was the perfect combination for us. He did many presentations and encouraged group projects.

The personalities of The Fab Five meshed in a way that was helpful when doing these group projects. One of the girls was very shy and soft-spoken. She liked to have things neat and organized, and when the teacher would lecture, she would quietly doodle in her notebook. Another girl was very social with an upbeat, positive attitude, and her peers loved to help her. Both boys were charming, easygoing, and willing to follow teachers' directions. One of these boys was a great artist, so if we ever needed to draw a picture, make a poster, or create sketches of something related to the science topic, he was the guy to do it. The third girl was an excellent self-advocate who needed encouragement in new situations. This was the perfect team of students to be in this class.

The regular education teacher was wonderfully inclusive and would have the students do current events with science-related themes. We would find the most interesting, earth-shattering things to report on, complete with pictures. We would write the summary of the article and practice in my class; then, each student took turns telling their discoveries. The other students were so kind and accepting, and my students were proud to be in this class. The teacher would give out an award for the most unusual current event, and we won that distinction several times that year.

We did a lot of projects for the big ideas in class. Once, we were tasked to explain the difference between mass and weight for the 6th-grade science class. This was a pretty advanced concept for my kids, but I always felt that incorporating music was a good teaching tool. I scoured the internet and discovered an incredible teacher who made videos of popular songs. I found a YouTube video posted on March 7, 2011, by Mr. Doug Edmonds called "The Mass vs. Weight Song" to the tune of "Sweet Caroline" (1969) composed by Neil Diamond. Mr. Edmonds wrote new lyrics to explain the difference between mass and weight. The Fab Five students loved learning the song, and when it was their turn to present, they got the entire 6th-grade science class to sing along with them. Who wouldn't want to break into the "ba ba ba" of that familiar chorus? It was a huge hit, and they all went home feeling like teachers themselves. They had taught the class a song that everyone would remember.

Samantha

Samantha took the school by storm when she arrived. With a quick temper and a high energy level, it would often take several people to get her out of compromising situations. She could say random things that left you wondering where they came from. When she ran into the wall one day, she said, "Well, that was a cranium collision!"

Another example was when the 8th graders went to a national cemetery. The dad of one of the students was buried there, and a flag was given to this student in memory of his father. Samantha got angry and said, "That's not fair! I want a flag too!" The aide took her aside and tried to explain the matter, and then she said, "Well, I wish my dad was dead too!" Fortunately, she was far enough away from everyone that no one else heard her outcry.

Samantha was uncoordinated and would often gallop down the halls without looking where she was going. This usually would result in her crashing into walls, other people, or, once, the volleyball net in PE class. She always had an aide with her because her working memory and spatial awareness were weak even though she was pretty high functioning. This served her well because if she was mad about something, she could walk with her aide and forget what had previously angered her.

She didn't really pay attention to how she looked in the morning, so we would quickly assess her style of the day and tell her to go into the restroom and turn her shirt the right way, put on two socks, or change out of the pants with holes. There always seemed to be some sort of clothing malfunction. Extra clothes in her size for such occasions were available. Still, she had a kind heart and was always eager to help others. I loved her enthusiasm and willingness to help other people.

Audrey

I had observed Audrey in elementary school, where the teacher said, "We have tried many things and are at a standstill right now." She would have meltdowns, resulting in the principal or another staff member taking her to a "cool down" place.

When I got her in 6th grade, I met with her parents to better understand what she was about. They had great insights and knew their daughter well. Dad likened her to a hot stove when she was in a heightened state, and you know, just to leave it alone until it cools down. This was very astute as a vivid description of her behavior. I tried to give her a safe space to cool down when she would lose control.

Sarcasm was almost a second language to her. When I asked her how she was feeling, she would reply, "Just fine, and I don't need your help." Once, she saw another student trip and fall and commented, "Well, that was fun." She did not do well if she was hungry, so I always had snacks. She could go from zero to sixty quickly, so the trick was to help her choose a snack before a meltdown. We knew her favorite snacks, but those would change as soon as a gust of wind blew through the town.

The cafeteria staff were wonderful with all my students and tried to provide their favorite food choices. If Audrey wanted breakfast, they made sure the breakfast bars she liked with banana and chocolate chips were available. She was a picky eater, and her food choices would change, so we needed a variety. Her parents provided snacks that were the current favorites at home. Once, the guidance counselor entered the room and saw she was upset. The counselor asked Audrey if she wanted a banana. "Do I look like a monkey?" she replied. Apparently, bananas were no longer on her list of favorite treats.

She would have a favorite food for a while, then it would change without warning. One of these go-to foods was chicken nuggets, and the cafeteria staff ensured they were available for Audrey. I had just finished reading with her and saw that she was starting to get "hangry," I better take action soon. I offered her a snack of her choice as a way to stave off the storm that was building in her. She refused, so I said, "Let's take a walk and see what the cafeteria offers." I knew they would have the winning choice of chicken nuggets which had been a favorite food up to this point. When we arrived, the head cafeteria lady asked sweetly, "Would you like chicken nuggets?" "F#@k Chicken Nuggets!" Audrey screamed, "I want a corn dog." I hate chicken nuggets, and I hate you!" "I'm sorry, honey, but we don't have any corn dogs," the patient and kind lunch lady explained. Audrey started to cry, and everyone around us looked horrified, including the lovely lunch lady just trying to appease Audrey. "Let's return to our class and see how the turtles are doing. I think they are hungry, and I was hoping you could feed them," I quietly whispered in her ear. I did not want to make more of a spectacle than what we already made. Thankfully, Audrey walked back to the room with me. She calmed down watching the turtles and willingly fed them.

Earlier that morning, Audrey saw another student get a pancake on a stick and thought it was a corn dog. The cafeteria did not have corn dogs, and Audrey felt it was a bait-and-switch situation. That day, no explaining or trying to appease her with other foods would work. Yogurt was her favorite snack choice. I ensured I always had that on hand so I could satisfy her with that.

I returned to the cafeteria and apologized to our head lunch lady. She laughed and said, "Well, that was unexpected!" I was grateful for her calm demeanor and willingness to help me. I appreciate her sense of humor as she now says to her husband, "F#@k (name a restaurant)!" if he suggests they go out to eat at a restaurant she doesn't like. Having a sense of humor is an excellent trait for times like these.

Audrey had a funny sense of humor and loved reading, so we started reading many books together and discussing them. We usually picked stories about flawed people or people who had overcome adversity. She loved this and began to thrive. She also started doing reader's theater pieces in my class, and she soared to the top of the class. We finally figured out a rhythm of working together, where she would do my required work and then have drawing time as a way to soothe herself.

I discovered she was very theatrical and did a great job memorizing lines. I talked her into trying out for the school musical. However, she became overwhelmed and did not do well in her tryout. The director (by then, I had retired from this position) was willing to give Audrey another chance in a very small group setting, but she did not try. I knew we would have to try again later, and she needed more time and space.

I found an online theater group for students on the spectrum that did workshops and classes to help her make connections and exhibit her abilities and gifts through empowerment. A former student belongs to this group, and I was impressed with their mission statement and saw plays that they did. Audrey continues to take classes from this group, and I hope she gains the confidence to try again to be on stage, as I believe she would do a fabulous job.

Audrey loved to read out loud, using different voices and superior inflection. She also was the perfect candidate to participate in the school's pre-recorded weekly morning announcements, telling a joke with another girl named Clara. This calm, quiet girl needed her self-confidence bolstered. The two girls worked very well together, and each week they would tell a joke as part of the weekly announcements. An example of their weekly routine is Audrey saying, "Why shouldn't you use a broken pencil?" Clara would respond, "I don't know, why?" Audrey would finish with, "Because it's pointless." She would laugh, and both girls felt a sense of pride.

Audrey loved all college mascots. You could ask her what the mascot was for any team, and she would tell you in detail what it looked like and how it acted. I would let her tell the class about different college mascots, and we would read articles about mascots as well. This was quite successful. She also loved TV shows with singing competitions, and I would also watch them so we could discuss the next day.

Audrey was such an interesting girl and grew socially, emotionally, and educationally when I had her. I loved discussing the books we read; she was usually very empathetic to the characters.

Ingrid

Ingrid was a girl with a big personality. She was a stubborn girl with Down syndrome who sometimes had difficulty complying with directions and sometimes had trouble transitioning from one activity to another. She was happiest when she was the show's star and loved the limelight. She liked to do things on her own timetable, in her own way.

As her teacher getting her ready to one day be employable, I knew we needed to work on compliance, being a team member, and transitions. An example was when it was time to leave her regular education science class, she did not want to leave with her aide. She loved being in the class, but the bell had rung, and it was time to go. The aide called me for help, and I went to the science class to see her spread-eagled on the science lab table holding the sides with a death grip. I remember looking at her, thinking, do we pull her from her arms or legs? We called her mom because we wanted to keep her safe, and pulling her off would cause potential harm and worse behavior. Mom promised her a reward for good behavior if she would comply, which she did. There were other times when she did not want to leave science class, and she was assisted by either of two brothers, who were also special education teachers. These two men were terrific allies and always willing to help redirect Ingrid. Many times, she would listen to a man instead of a woman.

The person she would listen to the most was the 6th-grade music teacher, Ms. Winter. Ingrid loved to sing and had a deep respect for her. I would call for her assistance even in 8th grade. Once, Ingrid decided not to come downstairs from the library and hid under one of the tables. It took a visit from Ms. Winter to convince her to come out from under the table.

We had a home/school behavior chart, and it started to be meaningful for her when there were rewards and consequences at home. Her parents were available to talk to her and give her little pep talks occasionally. These home chats resulted in her compliance, transition times became shorter, and she became more cooperative. She was energetic, friendly, and outgoing. She liked to have her way and would press on until she got it. She would refuse to do tasks at times. Still, as she matured, she learned strategies to help when frustrated, anxious, and needing sensory input. She was on the road to better life skills when she left for high school.

Bennie

Bennie was a boy with autism and quite the literal thinker. I knew that, but I would still have to watch myself when I would say things like "he seems to have a chip on his shoulder, let's put it in gear and get going" or "his head is in the clouds" for he would look at me as if I was speaking a foreign language. This is quite common for students like Bennie. To help him understand what idioms mean, we created a book. He would make pictures of the saying and what it really meant. For example, if the phrase was "His head is in the clouds," he would draw a picture of a person surrounded by clouds, and then below it would write, "he is being distracted with other thoughts." Visuals were a great way to help him. He was an expert on all things related to science-fiction movies and US Presidents. He loved reading about these topics, which were great motivators for him.

As we worked through the various idioms, it became clear that Bennie loved reading aloud to other people and sharing his writing. He used great inflection and spoke loudly and clearly. I knew he would be a great candidate when I was asked who would like to do the weekly joke-telling for the pre-recorded morning school announcements. I picked Bennie and Audrey to perform. They would tell knock-knock jokes which were perfect for the two of them, as he had a great, enthusiastic speaking voice. Even though Audrey was hard to understand at times, she too loved to perform, and when it was her turn, she said, "Who's there?" with enthusiasm and clarity. They were quite the dynamic duo and got asked to do it each week.

Jack

I was excited to learn I was getting Valerie's brother, Jack, in my class. She had been such a fun girl. Their mom, a former teacher, understood the challenges of teaching and always provided helpful insight as we worked together to decide the best plan for her daughter.

Jack's Individual Education Program from elementary school had words like loud, non-compliant, and physically aggressive. It went on to describe how he could be disruptive to the learning of others. I was curious and had to understand what worked best for him. I observed him, took careful notes, and listened carefully to the wise words of his teacher and the paraprofessionals who worked with him. They said he needed lots of space, so when he came to middle school, we created his own "office," complete with dividers, a desk with cubbies for materials, and the rocking chair he cherished from elementary school. He seemed very routine-oriented, so I tried to give him the repetitive structure he craved. He was used to working on three set tasks and then given a break. I maintained that same regimen.

Jack would do a lot of self-talking and comment on what others were doing in the class. I could always tell when he was tempted to lash out at someone, for his previous go-to behavior was to hit someone if they annoyed him. He would say, "No hitting," which let me know it was his temptation. I would go over to his seat and say, "That is a good idea, Jack. We don't hit our friends."

If someone else became upset, it would upset him. He was very in tune with what was happening in the class, even though looking at him, you would think his mind was somewhere else. He would say things like, "Audrey is sad," and then I knew I had to reassure him we were trying to help Audrey. Jack, like his sister, did not like to have threads on his clothing. I knew by experience to deal with them quickly before they became holes that quickly unraveled.

As a sixth grader, Jack worked on transitioning from elementary school and learning the new vocabulary of middle school. He wanted to know what each activity we were doing was called. If he didn't know, he would say things like, "It's time for circle time," and I would say, "We are doing our calendar activities." These were the middle school version of knowing calendar concepts of today, yesterday, and tomorrow, the weather, and what was on the day's agenda.

Jack had only attended a few regular education classes in elementary school. I found that he enjoyed music, science, and social studies classes. He would only know what he liked once he attended those classes, so I allowed him to experience different courses. Once he knew the routine and what was expected of him, he really looked forward to those classes and would tell me, "It is time for Health."

Jack always thought about something, but an idea might only come out several hours later. These ideas came out at the most random times. One time in choir, he blurted out, "We are in deep space." It was probably a thought he had from his morning science class. His aide looked at him and replied, "No, Jack, we are in the choir."

It seemed his brain was like a pinball machine, with ideas shooting out of his mouth like someone had pulled and released the shooter knob. To Jack, it was probably one of many thoughts running through his mind. There were things he missed, others caught, but there were also things he saw that others would miss. Sometimes when working with students with autism, we have to step back and teach in new ways that they can learn when traditional methods don't work for Jack. That meant always knowing what would happen and providing visual pictures of ideas whenever possible.

Jack's aide could not go with him on the day of the choir performance, so I went to the choir concert with him. I realized I had no idea what the actions of the songs were, and believe me, there were plenty of moves. We had the best choir teachers in the whole district. Two ladies were terrific with my students, taking them at whatever level they were and allowing them to perform. So here we were, in the middle of a performance, and I looked to the boy standing next to Jack for guidance. I soon realized I had nothing to fear, for Jack knew all the motions and all the words of the songs, which he sang perfectly.

In Health class, he would go every day and sit in his assigned seat. This teacher had a niece with Down syndrome and clearly understood my students and how to best help them. She welcomed them into her class, and we worked on big ideas for her class. One day the teacher changed the seating chart, and someone else was sitting in the seat Jack thought was his assigned seat. It had been before, and as I said, Jack did not like changes. A boy named Frankie was in the seat Jack thought belonged to him, so he tried to push him off the chair. When Jack's aide finally got him settled in his new seat, Jack said, "Frankie is wearing underwear." We learned that was one of the sayings he would say when he felt something was wrong. So and so (insert the name of whomever he was annoyed with) is wearing underwear became a warning to us to see what was wrong in his world and try to fix it or help him understand the right way to deal with the problem. This was an example of us learning to teach the way he knew. He tried to be a problem solver, but his way to problem solve was not always the right way. He lived in a world of order and rules, and once we understood his rules and order, the year became a great success.

One time the school had a fire drill, and one of the alarms was in my classroom. The fire drill sound went off, and we quickly exited the room. On the way out, Jack pulled our room's alarm, thinking he was shutting off the noise. We had to radio a confused front office to explain what he had done because our unaware custodian was trying to determine the real fire's source. No real fire, just Jack's problem-solving. We then knew we needed to move his "office" far from the alarm.

As time passed, and he understood expectations and knew he would have to do work but would have breaks, his whole demeanor changed. He was more willing to do non-preferred tasks and learned to problem-solve in more socially acceptable ways. Seeing him make substantial academic, social, and emotional strides was exciting.

Courtney

One year, one of the elementary teachers called and said, "We need to meet in person. I have a girl for you with autism named Courtney who will require special care." Every spring, I would observe all the incoming students at their elementary schools. I got students from three and sometimes four of the district elementary schools. I knew this meant multiple meetings to understand this girl. This would be more than the typical meeting of Here is your student and her needs. Courtney had been a new student in the middle of the school year, and everything the elementary teacher knew, she had to find out the hard way. There was no information other than an IEP that was written from another state; sometimes, those are hard to understand.

Courtney had a lot of anxiety and a very low tolerance for others. She did not like it when people hummed and talked too loud or too long. She would quickly become angry and spew words that would make a sailor blush. The teacher told me she needed her own "office." She said you could tell just by the look on Courtney's face when it would be a bad day, and at that point, she needed some cool-down strategies. Her calming activities included listening to music, coloring, and playing on the tablet. She loved all things about toy horses.

The summer before she became my student, I stocked up on coloring books, sticker books, and a good collection of toy horse items. I found a cute desk and made Courtney her "office" area, surrounding her with walled dividers for her privacy. I bought her a diary, new markers, and coloring pages to use as rewards. When she came to my school, she immediately took to the space I had created for her. She wanted it walled off, so I found a low divider so I could see her but give her a feeling of privacy. She was a great reader and liked to read, so we would have book chats together, then I would give her time to be by herself. Math was not her favorite activity, so I always let Courtney practice some computer skills before our individual lesson.

Courtney was a bright and curious learner, and it was time for her to try to be in some regular classes. I challenged her at first to be in the 6th-grade social studies class. The teacher was warm and welcoming, always making my students feel essential to the course. I went with her and said we would try to be in the class for ten minutes, then she could come back to my room and fill in a miniature horse coloring page. She agreed, and I set my timer.

After five minutes, she loudly asked me how much time we had left in this stupid class. The regular education teacher heard her and said he was glad she joined today's course. The other students did not react to her, which was quite helpful. The teacher knew ten minutes was my goal for that day, and I felt like we had a ticking time bomb. He asked her opinion on the discussion topic, and she gave him an intelligent, on-topic answer. She looked at me and said, "Are you happy?"

I replied, "I am ecstatic." She gave me the slightest smile, which was a huge win that day. She liked to learn new vocabulary words.

"What does that mean?" she inquired.

"It means I am pleased you met your goal," I replied.

"Now can we go back to our class?" she asked.

"Yes, you reached your goal today," I said.

"Tell me you're ecstatic," she replied.

"I am ecstatic," I said as I watched the grin form on her face. She calmly returned to my room with pride that she had met her goal.

Slowly, we increased her time in this class, and she began to like it. Next, she tried the Physical Education class. The teacher was very flexible, and she could do alternate activities if the activities were too complicated. When they had free time, I discovered Courtney loved to jump rope, and she was pretty good. We used that as a motivator for other activities that she did not like. I thought we were making significant progress, but she started yelling at me during PE one day. "I hate this class!" she blurted out as the class just received instructions for the period. "YOU ARE ALL A BUNCH OF IDIOTS!"

"What do you need?" I quietly whispered.

"YOU TO LEAVE ME ALONE!" she screamed. I knew we had to leave quickly before the situation escalated. She ran out of the room and back to our classroom. I trailed behind at a distance. She threw herself into her chair, into the safety of her office. I followed her and asked her what was wrong.

"Shut up, you ugly furball!" Did she just call me an ugly furball? Wow! I didn't know what to say but realized I should have let her cool down. I had never been called an ugly furball, and I must admit I was biting my lip to keep from laughing. In my mind, she definitely got points for originality. I let her have the time to cool down before I talked to her, but her outburst just seemed to come out of the clear blue sky.

When she would get angry, she would get angry at everyone. Her typical response was to call everyone a bunch of idiots. We worked on ways to destress without any name-calling. We practiced social stories and had a chart she could show me when she reached her boiling point.

Later, I realized she did not want to do the PE teacher's assigned activities and didn't even know we could do alternate activities. She tried to do exercises when she wanted to do them. So, the new goal became: she had to know she didn't get to do everything she wanted, that classes were full of give and take, and if she showed some degree of cooperation, she would be rewarded with the free time to enjoy the activities she preferred.

There were times when Courtney was upset with herself. However, she would not apologize for her behavior, which usually involved telling other people what they were doing wrong, that they were a bunch of idiots, and just leaving her alone.

Courtney always wanted to know exactly what I expected of her, so we started writing daily goals. She would tell me that I was her only friend. She craved my attention, and we would have great conversations when she was appropriate and calm. What I heard her saying in her own way was help me make friends. The first thing we discussed was how to say nice things to people.

I invited her to our group discussions for an activity called "The Friendship Circle." Sometimes she refused but would offer her input from the safety of her office. I knew she was listening, so I had other students model conversation starters and ways to be a good listener to others.

By her second year in my class, Courtney was going to regular education classes for more extended periods and would allow one of the aides to go with her instead of just me. One day she came back to my class early and was clearly upset. Two aides were walking with her, and one said, "Remember to use nice words!" so I knew things were going downhill quickly, and she needed to get to her cool-down chair.

Courtney looked at the other aide. The aide told her to use nice words. Courtney started sputtering, clearly trying to stay calm, and said, "You, you, you... not an idiot!!"

Knowing where she started in this journey, I viewed this as progress. Even though it was hard to show restraint, she did not use her go-to phrase by calling the aide an idiot. Being called "not an idiot" was a step in the right direction. She was now aware of what was spewing out of her mouth and began exercising some control. Sometimes progress is measured in small steps.

Courtney and I went to her general music class together. This was a wonderful experience for her, as the teacher was very engaging and had many interactive activities where kids could try different musical genres. They learned different rhythms by banging on 5-gallon buckets with drumsticks. They got to try instruments which were color-coded tuned plastic percussion tubes. Creating her own music spoke to her creative abilities, and working with the group and following directions were excellent skills for her to learn. Courtney was good at patterning and echoing and did not seem to mind the noise, which was unusual for her. She sang the folk songs we learned and participated in the fun ways the teacher would use to study for tests, like playing board games or making colored flash cards. When we began learning to play the guitar part of the class, she made friends with other students. She would leave the course in a good mood; if not, we would go early before she got too frustrated, so she stayed in a good mood. She taught me to really look at students and end a session of whatever he or she was doing before they became frustrated. Once again, it was a case of the teacher becoming the student. The timing was everything.

Kevin

Every student I had left an imprint on my heart, but one boy left a legacy of hope, heartache, and faith. Kevin was a boy who had Duchenne muscular dystrophy. This is a terrible disease that is characterized by progressive muscle degeneration. He was diagnosed at age four and lost the ability to walk at age eight. When he reached middle school, he was in a wheelchair but could move his hands and independently control his motorized chair. He would tire during the day, so he would take breaks, and we would talk. He never let muscular dystrophy define who he was. He had a beautiful spirit and was optimistic in the face of devastating circumstances. He taught me that God uses the simplest things in life to teach us lessons.

Even though Kevin was aware of his struggles and limitations, he faced them head-on and was a constant source of kindness and good cheer to all who knew him. Working hard in classes and thanking my aides and me for each simple thing we helped him with brought us a sense of gratitude to have this amazing boy in the class. Kevin loved superheroes, science fiction, and cars and would get excited about meeting new people.

He had to go on homebound instruction for a while, and I was the teacher to help him. Going to his house, I understood where he got his faith and optimism, for it was ingrained in the fabric of his whole family. He delighted in showing me all the pictures of cars on his bedroom wall. He showed me pictures of his adorable niece, and he was clearly a very proud uncle.

He attended a Discover Ohio program on three separate day trips in eighth grade. Kevin's aide made up a game for him in the gym of our recreation center to move a ball with his wheelchair. He loved it and was delighted when other kids came over to play his game too. We talked about high school, and Kevin said he couldn't wait to go to high school and see all those pretty girls.

He loved hanging out with friends, listening to music, and playing video games with them. Kevin had a wonderful best friend and met many wonderful people at the summer camp he went to called Camp Cheerful. In the three years, I had him in my class, he gradually lost the ability to feed himself, but that did not dampen his spirit. When we went outside for recess, this remarkable young man wanted to be around other kids no matter how cold. Kevin wanted to stay out as long as possible, and sometimes his hands would get so hard that he couldn't operate his chair, but he didn't care. Kevin never wanted to miss a moment. Maybe even then, he knew his time here on Earth was limited. He did but was determined to make the most of every day.

Kevin was presented with many challenges in his short life. When an aide had to help him eat, he thanked her each day. No matter how difficult his condition progressed, he would change his approach and find something good about the situation. He saw himself as a warrior hero, fighting a hero's battle against muscular dystrophy. He would tell me he wanted to maintain a good attitude, and this warrior hero did that gracefully.

As I helped his mom talk to the high school about his needs and what classes he should take, she said, "Let's give him the biggest party of all and put him in all the fun classes." She had tears in her eyes, and I had tears in mine. We signed Kevin up for the video class, knowing he would have a great experience, and put him in other highly engaging courses.

We celebrated every day, and he cherished his family and friends deeply. His best friend lived two doors away from him and developed a deep and pure friendship. Kevin could visit New York City and see the Statue of Liberty with his parents and best friend. He went to the Senior Prom with a girl. When this Warrior Hero graduated from high school, he wore his cap and gown and was wheeled across the stage to get his diploma.

People who knew Kevin all had their lives enriched and made better by this brave, courageous young man. Kevin was 20 years old when he passed away. When I went to the visitation, I reflected on the life lessons he taught all of us who were so blessed to know him. I picture him running free and flying high with the Angels. I feel like God used Kevin to remind us all to be open, honest and look for the best in everyone and everything. His life did not go unnoticed. We all became better people by the grace that allowed us to know this fine young man.

Cheryl

Dr. Stephen Shore said, "If you meet one student with autism, then you have met one student with autism." This was about how diverse individuals with autism are. I know this to be accurate, and the same could be said about students with any other disability. A myth about people with Down syndrome is that they are always happy. Still, people with Down syndrome have feelings and moods like everyone else.

Cheryl had Down syndrome and was in my class for three years. She was reticent and shy and had a lot of social anxiety. One day this quiet little girl was sitting at her desk, clearly unhappy to almost tears. I asked her what was bothering her, and she said she was sad because her friend Josh was sad. Empathy is the ability to understand and share another person's feelings, and this little girl in my class with Down syndrome showed how empathetic she could be.

Cheryl also collected pencils and was known to quietly take all the pencils that were left at student desks. She would look for them on the floor and occasionally take more than one out of the community pencil basket. Her mom was aware of this habit and told me to check her pencil case and remove some. She would also send in full plastic bags of pencils that Cheryl had somehow absconded in her quiet, stealthy manner. She made me laugh because she was so quiet and, at first glance, was very compliant. Later, I realized she would take pencils and claim them as hers. Cheryl had a very orderly mind and loved to organize things. Having that many pencils helped her to organize other tangible items. She would make a great office worker one day if she could learn to leave other people's pencils alone.

Cheryl loved a popular children's movie and would sign using the lead character's name as her own. She loved to talk about her family and her cat, and she loved to play with children's movie toy characters. She made me realize that each person with Down syndrome has different talents and the ability to thrive.

Blake and Todd

Two boys with autism were tuned in to other people's feelings. One boy named Blake would look at Cheryl and say, "Cheryl is feeling sad." Frequently he would pick up on her moods before I would. The other boy named Todd would also notice changes in the behaviors of other students. He might say, "Cheryl is happy." Both of these boys were very artistic, and when I would read to them, they would draw insightful and thoughtful drawings about what they heard. They became friends, and it was always interesting that they were in tune with emotions.

Dwayne

Dwayne was a joyful boy with Down syndrome that loved to dance. His favorite song was "Happy" written and sung by Pharrell Williams (2013). My husband downloaded it on my music account, so I could pull it up to listen whenever I felt the class needed a break. Dwayne would ask to hear the song after we got our work done. I happily complied. Dwayne had great dance moves and inspired everyone in the class to move. Every time I hear that song, I still think of him and the unbridled joy he felt when he danced.

When he came to my sixth-grade class, I could see that having friends in and out of my room was very important to him. Everyone liked him, and students would high-five him as he went down the hall. When the sixth-grade class decided to have a float for the homecoming parade, Dwayne and I rode it together, and his enormous grin showed satisfaction. I realized kids liked him because he was always happy and wanted to be involved in class activities.

For Halloween, the PTO had a fundraiser that included treats, dancing, and a haunted house. Kids got to go in costume. I knew Dwayne would want to go, so I ensured his mom got the information about the party. I decided to go too and help him navigate the party, but once he got to the gym, where they had music, he wouldn't go any further. Dwayne was in his happy place of non-stop dancing. I suggested he stop and drink water, but he refused to take a break. Seeing the sweat run down Dwyane's forehead, I began to get worried. He needed a break, and it was time to try a different approach. I explained the situation to the DJ, asking if they could take a break. Once they stopped the music, Dwayne finally rested and got a drink of water.

Special Olympics Field Day

Every spring, my students participated in a Special Olympics field day. It was a day spent outside at a local high school where everyone got to compete. Much pomp and circumstance occurred in the Miracle League baseball style, starting with a parade of athletes in the opening ceremony. The physical education teachers would help us with this event, and Dwayne was in his glory. Not only did he like to dance, but he liked any physical activity.

Special Olympics Field Day was one of my favorite days of the year. We would practice in the gym and take time trials to submit so that the athletes were put in the correct heats. Our school's two physical education teachers would greatly help me as they helped organize the kids into events. Track and field events included relay races, individual races, softball throw, and long jump. If students needed a buddy, one was available. If someone was in a wheelchair, there was an additional event called ramp roll, where the person put a ball on a ramp and rolled down the field. This event was for both middle and high school, so we would see our former students compete. Students from nearby schools were also invited, and the day was filled with festivities such as face painting, balloon art, crafts, and mascots from our Cleveland professional sports teams. Parents filled the football stadium stands, proudly taking the entire week before the big event. I would use it as a time to bring awareness to my school.

My principal was on board for this venture, so every morning, all the homerooms were shown various videos featuring the amazing things that people with disabilities could do. Some videos were from previous years at the Special Olympics Games, featuring talented Special Olympics athletes worldwide. Some of the videos were people with special needs describing their wants and desires to make everyone realize that everyone has the exact basic needs. Some of my favorite videos had people with various disabilities saying, "We are more alike than different."

A festive, celebratory atmosphere was present from the minute we got off our school bus at the high school football field of the event. Different schools would take turns hosting the event. As in the actual Olympics, student-athletes lined up and marched in a parade of athletes with fans in the stadium cheering them on. It was indeed a day of celebration and fun.

Lunches were donated on the event day, and every school had their same-colored t-shirt, so teams were quickly recognized. Everyone was given a medal for each event and felt pride in their victories. It was a day of triumph and festivity, with the day's theme being the Special Olympic Oath, "Let me win, but if I cannot win, let me be brave in the attempt." As we rode the bus back to our school, each student proudly looked at their medals. They felt like they had won a gold medal in the National Olympics.

COVID-19

During the spring of the first wave of the COVID-19 Global pandemic, my class and the whole school went to virtual learning. This was a considerable challenge and steep learning curve to learn how to teach online and how to engage my students in a new way that would hold their attention. I watched countless how-to videos to understand how to lead in this new way. For the most part, most of my students did a great job attending all of the online Internet sessions. I would meet daily with them to make sure not only their educational needs were being met but their social and emotional needs were met as well.

This was a whole new frontier, and there wasn't a lot of guidance on how to navigate this new virtual world. At times it felt like learning to fly while in the air as we were building the airplane. I knew I needed to be creative and innovative to hold their attention. I learned how to record myself reading a fun book and got copies for all the students to read along. We tried to create more real-world math problems, and I was so pleased with my students' initiative. They had a choice of doing a project, dressing like a character, or writing something about the book as one of their projects. They could draw pictures to share with the rest of the class or make a fort using building blocks to show their understanding of the book. I realized a huge part of the success was the support of the parents, and I was blessed to have parents dedicated to continuing their child's learning. I had to laugh when I would hear a mom or dad say, "Pay attention. Look at the teacher!" It was fantastic to have such amazing parents. It was a team effort, and I wanted to find a way to celebrate my students and let them have something special for all their hard work.

We live in a suburb of Cleveland, so I asked if the local professional baseball team mascot could join us in a virtual video meeting. I had some big baseball fans and a girl who generally loved mascots in my room. It was set up and became one of our favorite experiences of the school year, with all of us joining, including parents, students, and caregivers. We also invited other teachers and their families to join us. We danced with the mascot and joined in a chorus of "Take Me Out to the Ballgame." My students could ask questions, listen to fun facts and practice their social skills in a whole new way. Seeing the joy on their faces brought great satisfaction as we navigated this new virtual world together.

The occupational therapist and I facilitated a project to help with coping skills and strengthen appropriate responses to frustrations with a specialized program. We had a virtual classroom via the internet with fun videos and songs. We read stories to the students about ways to foster self-control and have the opportunity to work on social-emotional learning. We would discuss the different zones of blue, green, yellow, and red each week and how to recognize different feelings with tools to cope with each emotion. It was a great time to carve out an important aspect of learning and an excellent way to check in with each student to make sure they felt connected without feeling isolated. We wanted to dedicate some understanding of mental health, an essential part of the road to success.

Even though it was a huge success for most, a couple of students would never log on or join in the learning. I gave those students paper/pencil tasks and delivered them to their homes. I knew there were a couple of students I did not reach in that springtime of online learning.

In the fall of the next school year, the school remained online at first, but it was determined by our school district that my students, and the rest of the district students with intensive needs, would be back in school. How could this be? It didn't make sense to me. I taught the most vulnerable population in the school and didn't feel like it was a safe thing to do. I am a professional, so when I was told, "Your class is going back in person," my students and I went back in person. I always look for the silver lining, so the silver lining in this was that we were the only ones in school. We could take mask breaks (yes, we had to wear masks) in the gym and had the outdoor picnic table shelter area to ourselves. There were times we went outside, safely distanced, and were able to learn our lessons outside. I made sure students knew all the ways to keep safe and healthy. We practiced the correct way of hand washing with illustrated pictures on a poster I made to remind everyone. Those two students I could not reach in the spring became active learners again. One was a girl who just needed the structure of learning in school.

Marissa

Marissa was an adorable, motherly girl with a mature outlook and a funny sense of humor. When we were online, I would call her, telling her it was time for school and she needed to do these computer-based learning problems. She would say things like," I have to walk my dog," or "I have to babysit my nieces." This was probably true in her mind, and she could only think of the immediate here-and-now environment of her family. Her mom had to work long hours and could not help her, and extended family members were living with her. I knew the distractions were real for her. Once she returned to school, she became a great student again. It didn't take me long to realize that in-person learning was the best for all of my students, and even though I considered our online learning a success, this was a better fit for all students.

Marissa loved to talk to the aides and me during our mask breaks. She had some excellent insights into other students' academic success. One time when one of the boys complained about all the work he had to do, she said, "You better learn to do it now because it is not going to get any easier."

Such words of wisdom came from her mouth. Marissa continued to be a motherly figure to the other students, redirecting them with sage words such as, "You need to just do it!"

My favorite times were when Marissa felt the frustration adults would think of from time to time. Whether it be someone refusing to work, being rude, or just being obstinate, she would say, "Lord, Help me, Jesus!" Her incredulous look made me feel like she could read my mind. This was exactly what we were all thinking, but coming out of her mouth made it extra sweet. Marissa had wisdom beyond her years, and having her in the class created a blanket of calm in the room. Sometimes she would call someone out on their behavior in a way that I could not do, and because it came from her, the response was tremendous. Her love of helping others and deep understanding of the frustrations of adults made her an excellent addition to the class. To this day, I sometimes look at situations that I feel are ridiculous and say, "Lord, Help me, Jesus!" Somehow, that always makes me feel better, thinking of the wisdom of sweet Marissa.

Sally

Sally was a girl who was short in stature but long in attention-seeking ways to be in the spotlight. She thrived when she got to do a presentation in class and was happiest when telling other students what they should be doing. This made Marissa very helpful because she would call Sally out, saying, "Sally, you are not the one in charge!"

Sally's Mom and I decided the best course of action would be to put Sally on a home-school report. Sometimes she got carried away with trying to be in the limelight, which would interfere with the teacher's directions. Once, a boy told her to be quiet, and when she thought no one was looking, she raised her middle finger at him slowly and deliberately. This is just one example of the very covert behaviors she would use to get attention. When I called her out, "Sally! Stop that!", she immediately knew she had been caught.

Sally's sneaky ways to get attention increased, so I knew I needed a new plan. Because she was an attention-seeking student, being in the spotlight was highly motivating for her. I added her to the group of students who got to be recorded making a joke for the morning announcements. She would be paired weekly with a no-nonsense boy who was very serious about this job. They would present a knock-knock joke, with him starting out and then Sally replying. She loved doing this and got to be center stage for good behavior. We used this as an incentive to get happy faces on her daily report. This helped tremendously, and I learned that it is important to celebrate each student's gifts, primarily when it works within the classroom. Pairing her with a no-nonsense, "I am not going to buy into your behavior type, boy" was a perfect fit. They were quite the dynamic duo and would often go down to the office and practice their jokes for the secretaries of our school. These ladies were a great and encouraging audience. Sally learned she got more attention when she did the right things and followed directions.

Mario

Mario was the youngest of four brothers and loved watching and playing sports. Growth and development were challenging for him as a baby born prematurely, and he had multiple doctor and therapy appointments during his first three years of life. He was diagnosed with 13Q deletion and mild cerebral palsy at age three. This 13Q is a chromosomal deletion that brings a variety of lifelong medical and developmental concerns.

When Mario was in sixth grade, one of the brothers was in eighth grade. This brother was a popular football player, and his friends would each make it a point to say hi and fist-bump Mario with that sort of bonding athletes often do. Everywhere he went, students would greet him. His mom once told me he was like the elementary school's mayor, which was also true in middle school. He was always ready to work and helpful to his peers, whether they needed a pencil, a piece of paper, or a door held open for them. He was the biggest cheerleader for any type of competition in our class, and his upbeat, cheerful demeanor was an instant mood booster for the students in my class. As an avid athlete, he plays any sport presented to him and cheers on everyone competing in the game.

Mario loved comics and action figures and loved to take on the persona of his favorite superheroes. He had so much love for these characters and liked to educate me on their strengths and abilities. He would walk down the hall and start making hand gestures which, of course, prompted me to ask him what he was doing. He would then tell me which superhero he was emulating. Oh, I got it; he was in his fantasy world. That was the fun thing about him. He loved these characters so much that he could transport himself to a scene of one of the superheroes and become that character. Every class should have someone who views himself as the mayor, can become a superhero, or is the biggest cheerleader for all his friends. I was the lucky one who got to have all three characters in one person.

He started in the band as a percussion player in sixth grade. He is now in high school and continues playing in the marching band. Imagine the pride I felt watching him march in the Memorial Day parade, not missing a beat and keeping perfect focus. He thrives daily and continues encouraging and supporting every sports team member or band member.

Alex

In the last year of my teaching career, we decided as a class that we needed a theme song; some song to greet everyone as they walked into my classroom. A boy named Alex loved a popular television show, so to make him smile, I started playing the show's theme song, "Thank You for Being a Friend." It seemed perfect for all of us. Mario sang along each day with his usual gusto, as if he was at a rock concert and Alex, a boy with apraxia and limited speech abilities, would have the biggest smile. We would put it on our smart board to watch a video clip from the show, then sing along with the person who originally sang it. It was the perfect way to start the day.

Alex was very personable and easygoing when he knew what to expect. He loved being a helper in the class, so I looked for jobs for him to do in school. We borrowed a three-wheeled bicycle from one of the elementary special education teachers for the year, and he made deliveries to various parts of our building. It became part of his routine to stop in the office twice a day, once in the morning and once in the afternoon, to see if any deliveries would be made. This worked out well for him because he was an active boy who needed lots of activities, and it strengthened his functional life curriculum. Once a day, he would get the laundry from the laundry room with his aide, fold the towels and return the basket to the cafeteria. At the end of the day, he would pick up and wash the dirty laundry. He learned to do these things independently, and when there was a substitute aide, he could show that person that he knew all the steps and the routine of the task. He loved to help where he could.

My class did a monthly pre-order lunch for the staff to teach life skills and generate funds for an end-of-the-year activity. It was a program that my daughter, who came into our class to work on occupational therapy goals, helped me create. Each month Alex and the other students helped make the meal, package it for delivery, and then deliver it to the staff who had previously ordered. Sometimes we would use our shopping cart to make deliveries. We made cute monthly order blanks with the menu items and delivered them to all the staff of our school who placed orders. Our meals included grilled cheese and soup, lasagna, chili, chicken salad, and other soups and side dishes. Alex loved participating in the process and was a great delivery person. Many skills were developed with this program we called "Time to Dine with 109" because our room number was 109. Students learned how to make simple lunches, kitchen safety, customer service, and money skills.

This was a program that Alex looked forward to each month and helped fulfill his need to be a part of a helping community.

At the end of the school year, we would have money from this program to do something special for the students. Several years ago, we had a traveling zoo come to our class. The students loved interacting with the birds, reptiles, and furry animals during this program. Each student wanted to come up and hold the giant snake, pet the tortoise, or get the myna bird to speak. Since I had two students who were blind, they were delighted to participate in this activity. We went bowling a couple of times at the end of the year and used the funds to learn how to make pizzas at a town square pizza shop or cupcakes at the cupcake shop. This program provided the funds to do many new and educational activities.

Jose

Jose was a boy who could be the most helpful and kind person in the room or the angriest, impulsive, and disobedient student in the class. He was a street-smart guy who didn't always attend school on time. Also, you never knew which version of Jose was coming to school. I previously had his older brother and sisters in my class, knew the family, and knew circumstances were beyond his control. I knew that he, like his brother, really liked animals, which would be a great connection for us to begin our relationship. Because I had spent my first years of teaching working with students with behavioral and emotional disabilities, I knew I had many tools I could use to help him.

Jose struggled with reading and was a strong hands-on learner, so I let him build or create whenever possible. I knew he didn't always meet his basic needs, so I always had snacks and a quiet room where he could work. Food and a sense of peace and quiet were essential to him. I loved having him in class.

Another tool to help Jose was working with him in a small group. I used the fact that he liked to help other students as a way to get him to work on his reading skills. I would tell him I needed his help to read along with Mario, a student he perceived as slower than himself. They were actually at the same reading level. Still, by combining his willingness to help others with a way to practice for himself, we strengthened his reading skills. He simply didn't show up when we had online learning, even though he was given a tablet to use at home. He was not an independent learner, so he could move forward with his basic skills when we returned to school in person.

Jose was the younger brother of the student I had to whom I gave the snapping turtle, and he also liked turtles. There is a high school counselor that previously worked at my school, and he loves turtles as well. He owns many land and water turtles and tortoises and is an expert. In the spring, there was a fire at his barn, and sadly, two of his giant African tortoises were affected. One died immediately, and the other was transported to a veterinary clinic, where he received alternating oxygen and hypertonic saline treatments to clear out the congestion in his lungs.

Because my students were animal lovers and knew our friend, the counselor, we decided to do a fundraiser in my class to help defray the cost of the vet bills. This cause was very important to Jose, and he became a leader in helping make posters for the fundraiser. We served coffee, tea, and wrapped cookies that staff in our school could purchase. My daughter donated homemade dog treats to sell. We had pictures of Terry, the tortoise, and the newspaper clipping that told what had happened and the treatments given. We asked Mr. White, the counselor, to come to the class. He had no idea this was an event we had created for him. He spoke to Jose personally, and they talked about turtles, tortoises, and their care. After Jose had left, I explained to Mr. White that he was an at-risk student and loved reptiles. Mr. White had worked with the older brother and sister, knew the family, and said he would be happy to connect with Jose once he went to high school. That made me feel so much better for Jose because I knew he would need all the friends and support he could get.

I was happy to find out that when Jose went to high school, one of our teachers of students with emotional disabilities decided to teach at the high school and would be able to work with Jose. She was young, enthusiastic, and worked well with at-risk students, so I was happy he would have a great start to high school. Having these two adults as his allies gave me hope for Jose. I tried to provide him with the best support I could possibly give with these two amazing adults ready to help him.

CHAPTER 10

Wrapping Up 42 Years of Teaching

Finding ways to help others and working on daily living skills were two crucial parts of the lessons I taught my students. They weren't part of any academic standards set by the State. Still, I felt like they were things I needed to teach my students so that they could become productive, helpful citizens of the world with as much independence as they could.

We started a school garden, and for the first few years, we would grow the plants from seeds, beginning with a grow light. Each student would help and take turns watering the plants. In May, we would make the seedlings hardier by putting them outside a few hours at a time. This outdoor exposure made the plants more robust and more resilient.

I would read the book, "S*eedfolks*" by Paul Fleischman to them as we worked on the project. It is a beautiful book filled with diverse characters from all walks of life. It is set in Cleveland, and we could relate since we live in Ohio. The people learn to work the land and become a community. I would tie it into our lessons, telling them that is what we were doing as well.

The day came near the end of May when we would transplant these plants into a raised garden bed. We had tomatoes, zucchini, peppers, and flowers. Each student would help plant the garden and take turns watering it for the rest of the year. In the fall, we would make salsa with tomatoes, and everyone would get to take some home. We would share it with the food bank if there was enough bounty. The lessons of helping others were reinforced. We, like the folks in the book, had become a community. By planting this garden together, my students learned the value of working together for a common goal.

One of the local nursing homes is a County Home, and the residents were the people who had the fewest visitors, some of them having disabilities themselves. I picked this nursing home as the one we would start building friendships with because I felt they had the greatest need. My class started doing monthly projects to make and share items like seasonal placemats, a candy wreath at Christmas, writing notes to them, and other favors we would make in class. It was a great connection to the community, and we often received letters of gratitude. One of the most rewarding times was when I took my students there to the County Home, and they played Bingo with the residents. One lady told me she loved getting our cards, so I ensured the students would do that often. Every month, we would get thank you cards from them that I would share with the students, then have them write letters back to the residents.

I was the co-sponsor of our school's service group, Builder's Club, with another teacher. This service organization's parent organization is the Kiwanis, a group of volunteers dedicated to helping build student leaders. This was an excellent opportunity to invite my students to be part of a group that would help others with monthly projects. From making fleece blankets to having a canned food drive and other service projects, all students can join their peers to work toward community service.

I learned early in my career the value of having my students join groups of other students, and I could make sure that happened when I was the adult in charge. Friendships were made, acceptance and understanding occurred, and everyone felt like they were contributing to a cause of helping others. All students, regardless of their ability, have similar wants and needs. They all need engaging learning strategies, inspiring role models, and proper lesson guidance. They need to have as many chances to succeed as necessary. They all want to have a feeling of belonging, of having friends, and of a sense that they are part of a larger community. Being in clubs and helping others are great ways to help people feel fulfilled.

I learned many life lessons from working with these students. I always tried to teach the big idea of concepts and subjects. At the beginning of this book, I wondered who learned more, me or my students. We all had things to learn from lessons that would become great life lessons. I feel blessed that I had a career doing what I loved and learned some big ideas along the way. These lessons can be valuable to anyone lucky enough to encounter kids with special needs. They have many lessons to teach us if we listen and learn. Here are ten big ideas I have learned and hopefully taught my students:

1. Success can only sometimes be measured by large steps. Slow and steady wins the race. Small steps, taken one at a time, can lead to achieving big goals.

2. It is vital to have a sense of humor when teaching. Sometimes humor can diffuse even highly tense situations. It helps increase student attention span and helps them retain learning.

3. Taking breaks and getting your wiggles out from time to time is essential. When we can move and take a break, we can become more productive. It could be as simple as walking down the hall to drink water.

4. Dancing can make us feel happy, calm and reduce stress. Dancing can serve as a break from the task at hand, and then you are ready to return to work.

5. Music is a way to make connections to people, places, and ideas. Some of the best lessons came with a song to sing. Music strengthens learning and memory and makes us happier.

6. There are different types of intelligence, and we should learn to teach to a person's strength. All children develop their own

motivations and talents at their own pace. Every person is different, and each of us has varying capabilities in these various intelligence types.

7. It is paramount to become community helpers, always looking for ways to help others. This enables students to have better social interaction, improves their self-esteem, and distracts them from their problems.

8. The most important lessons don't come from books but come from the heart. When students learn to play fair, communicate with others, think of others, and listen to others, they learn from the heart.

9. When kids find someone to help, they also help themselves. Being a helper can improve self-esteem and give the helper a sense of purpose and self-worth.

10. Everyone should feel celebrated and be given recognition for their gains. Not everyone is going to college, but when people are celebrated for achieving their personal goals, endorphins are released inside their bodies, and they can feel incredible.

These were the truths I learned when teaching my students through the years. They are truths that every person going into teaching should know, and they won't always be found in college courses. Teaching is a journey of self-discovery, and in teaching these students, I discovered that they taught me to be a better person. These students enriched my life, and I am grateful to have found a path I loved. I hope one day you can also have the privilege of knowing some special people in your life. You will become enlightened and blessed in many ways.

Made in the USA
Monee, IL
09 October 2023

44260834R00083